50 Japanese Pizza Recipes for Home

By: Kelly Johnson

Table of Contents

- Okonomiyaki Pizza
- Teriyaki Chicken PIzza
- Miso Eggplant Pizza
- Sushi Pizza
- Japanese Curry Pizza
- Soba Noodle Pizza
- Wasabi Mayo Shrimp Pizza
- Sesame Beef Yakiniku Pizza
- Mentaiko and Shiso Pizza
- Matcha Dessert Pizza
- Yuzu Salmon Pizza
- Japanese Mushroom Pizza
- Ginger Pork Gyoza Pizza
- Ginger Pork Gyoza Pizza
- Edamame and Avocado Pizza
- Wakame Seaweed Pizza
- Yakitori Chicken Skewer Pizza
- Japanese Plum (Ume) Pizza
- Sesame-Crusted Tofu Pizza
- Nikujaga Beef Pizza
- Soy-Glazed Shitake Pizza
- Sakura Cherry Blossom Pizza
- Mochi and Red Bean Pizza
- Yuzu Kosho Shrimp Pizza
- Shabu-Shabu Beef Pizza
- Tempura Veggie Pizza
- Soy-Glazed Black Cod Pizza
- Tamago (Japanese Omelette) Pizza
- Mushroom Miso Butter Pizza
- Yakitori Quail Egg Pizza
- Soba Salad Pizza
- Japanese Pumpkin (Kabocha) Pizza
- Teriyaki Tofu and Broccoli Pizza

- Sesame-Crusted Salmon Pizza
- Yuzu-Honey Chicken Pizza
- Japanese Pickles Pizza
- Tonkatsu Pork Pizza
- Soy-Ginger Scallops Pizza
- Natto and Shiso Pizza
- Sesame Asparagus and Egg Pizza
- Miso Maple Bacon Pizza
- Ginger Miso Chicken Pizza
- Yuzu Pepper Tuna Tataki Pizza
- Wasabi Edamame Hummus Pizza
- Sukiyaki Beef and Onion Pizza
- Yakitori Pineapple Teriyaki Pizza
- Udon Noodle Pizza
- Match White Chocolate Dessert Pizza
- Tofu Katsu Pizza
- Yakitori Beef and Shishito Pepper Pizza

Okonomiyaki Pizza

Ingredients:

For the Okonomiyaki Pizza Base:

- 1 pizza dough (store-bought or homemade)
- 1 cup shredded cabbage
- 1/2 cup sliced green onions
- 1/2 cup tenkasu (tempura scraps)
- 1/2 cup cooked and diced bacon or pork belly
- 1/4 cup pickled red ginger (beni shoga)
- 1/4 cup mayonnaise
- 2 tablespoons Okonomiyaki sauce
- 1 tablespoon soy sauce
- 1 teaspoon sesame oil

Toppings (Optional):

- Bonito flakes (katsuobushi)
- Aonori (seaweed flakes)
- Sesame seeds

Instructions:

Preheat Oven:
- Preheat your oven according to the pizza dough package instructions.

Prepare Okonomiyaki Base:
- In a bowl, combine shredded cabbage, sliced green onions, tenkasu, diced bacon or pork belly, and pickled red ginger.

Sauce Mixture:
- In a small bowl, mix mayonnaise, Okonomiyaki sauce, soy sauce, and sesame oil to create the sauce mixture.

Roll Out Pizza Dough:
- Roll out the pizza dough on a floured surface to your desired thickness.

Assemble Pizza:
- Place the rolled-out dough on a pizza stone or baking sheet.
- Spread a generous amount of the sauce mixture over the dough.
- Evenly distribute the Okonomiyaki base over the sauced dough.

Bake:

- Follow the pizza dough package instructions for baking. Typically, bake in a preheated oven until the crust is golden and toppings are cooked.

Optional Toppings:
- Once out of the oven, sprinkle bonito flakes, aonori, and sesame seeds over the pizza for an extra layer of flavor and texture.

Serve:
- Slice the Okonomiyaki Pizza into portions and serve hot.

Enjoy the unique and delicious combination of Okonomiyaki flavors on a pizza crust!

Feel free to customize the toppings to suit your taste preferences.

Teriyaki Chicken PIzza

Ingredients:

For the Teriyaki Chicken:

- 1 pound boneless, skinless chicken breasts, sliced into thin strips
- 1/2 cup teriyaki sauce
- 2 tablespoons soy sauce
- 1 tablespoon mirin (Japanese sweet rice wine)
- 1 tablespoon sugar
- 1 teaspoon minced garlic
- 1 teaspoon grated ginger

For the Pizza:

- 1 pizza dough (store-bought or homemade)
- 1 cup shredded mozzarella cheese
- 1/2 cup sliced red bell pepper
- 1/2 cup sliced green bell pepper
- 1/2 cup sliced red onion
- 2 tablespoons sesame seeds (for garnish)
- 2 green onions, sliced (for garnish)

Instructions:

Preheat Oven:
- Preheat your oven according to the pizza dough package instructions.

Marinate Chicken:
- In a bowl, combine the teriyaki sauce, soy sauce, mirin, sugar, minced garlic, and grated ginger.
- Add the sliced chicken to the marinade, ensuring it's well coated. Let it marinate for at least 15-20 minutes.

Cook Teriyaki Chicken:
- In a skillet over medium heat, cook the marinated chicken until fully cooked and the sauce has thickened, about 5-7 minutes. Set aside.

Roll Out Pizza Dough:
- Roll out the pizza dough on a floured surface to your desired thickness.

Assemble Pizza:
- Place the rolled-out dough on a pizza stone or baking sheet.

- Spread a thin layer of teriyaki sauce (from the cooked chicken) over the dough.
- Evenly distribute the cooked teriyaki chicken over the sauced dough.
- Add shredded mozzarella cheese, sliced red and green bell peppers, and red onion on top.

Bake:
- Follow the pizza dough package instructions for baking. Typically, bake in a preheated oven until the crust is golden, and the cheese is melted and bubbly.

Garnish:
- Sprinkle sesame seeds and sliced green onions over the baked pizza for added flavor and presentation.

Serve:
- Slice the Teriyaki Chicken Pizza into portions and serve hot.

Enjoy the delicious combination of teriyaki chicken and pizza flavors in every bite! Customize with your favorite vegetables or additional toppings as desired.

Miso Eggplant Pizza

Ingredients:

For the Miso Glazed Eggplant:

- 2 medium-sized eggplants, sliced into 1/2-inch rounds
- 2 tablespoons white miso paste
- 2 tablespoons mirin (Japanese sweet rice wine)
- 1 tablespoon soy sauce
- 1 tablespoon sesame oil
- 1 tablespoon rice vinegar
- 1 teaspoon grated ginger
- 2 cloves garlic, minced

For the Pizza:

- 1 pizza dough (store-bought or homemade)
- 1 cup shredded mozzarella cheese
- 1/2 cup crumbled feta cheese
- 1/4 cup sliced green onions
- 1 tablespoon sesame seeds (for garnish)
- Fresh cilantro or parsley for garnish (optional)

Instructions:

Preheat Oven:
- Preheat your oven according to the pizza dough package instructions.

Prepare Miso Glaze:
- In a small bowl, whisk together white miso paste, mirin, soy sauce, sesame oil, rice vinegar, grated ginger, and minced garlic.

Marinate Eggplant:
- Brush each side of the eggplant slices with the miso glaze.
- Place the marinated eggplant slices on a baking sheet lined with parchment paper.

Roast Eggplant:
- Roast the eggplant in the preheated oven for about 15-20 minutes or until they are tender and golden brown. Flip the slices halfway through the cooking time.

Roll Out Pizza Dough:

- Roll out the pizza dough on a floured surface to your desired thickness.

Assemble Pizza:
- Place the rolled-out dough on a pizza stone or baking sheet.
- Evenly distribute the roasted miso-glazed eggplant slices over the pizza dough.
- Sprinkle shredded mozzarella cheese and crumbled feta cheese over the eggplant.

Bake:
- Follow the pizza dough package instructions for baking. Typically, bake in a preheated oven until the crust is golden, and the cheese is melted and bubbly.

Garnish:
- Sprinkle sliced green onions and sesame seeds over the baked pizza.
- Optionally, garnish with fresh cilantro or parsley.

Serve:
- Slice the Miso Eggplant Pizza into portions and serve hot.

Enjoy the delightful combination of miso-glazed eggplant and cheesy goodness! Feel free to experiment with additional toppings or drizzle with extra miso glaze for more flavor.

Sushi Pizza

Ingredients:

For the Sushi Rice "Crust":

- 2 cups sushi rice, cooked and seasoned with rice vinegar, sugar, and salt
- Nori (seaweed) sheets, cut into small rounds (to mimic pizza crust)
- Sesame seeds for garnish

For the Toppings:

- Sashimi-grade fish (e.g., tuna, salmon), thinly sliced
- Avocado, sliced
- Cucumber, julienned
- Tobiko (fish roe) for garnish
- Soy sauce and wasabi for serving

For the Sauce:

- 1/4 cup mayonnaise
- 1 tablespoon Sriracha sauce (adjust to taste)
- 1 teaspoon soy sauce
- 1 teaspoon sesame oil

Instructions:

Prepare Sushi Rice Crust:
- Press a thin layer of seasoned sushi rice onto small, individual nori rounds, forming a crust. You can use a mold or shape it by hand.

Make the Spicy Mayo Sauce:
- In a small bowl, mix together mayonnaise, Sriracha sauce, soy sauce, and sesame oil. Adjust the spice level to your liking.

Assemble Sushi Pizza:
- Spread a thin layer of the spicy mayo sauce over each sushi rice crust.

Add Toppings:
- Arrange slices of sashimi-grade fish, avocado slices, and julienned cucumber on top of the spicy mayo-covered sushi rice.

Garnish:
- Sprinkle tobiko over the toppings for a burst of color and additional flavor.
- Garnish with sesame seeds for extra texture.

Serve:
- Carefully transfer the sushi pizzas to serving plates.
- Serve with soy sauce and wasabi on the side for dipping.

Enjoy:
- Dig in and enjoy your Sushi Pizza by grabbing a slice with chopsticks or your hands!

Feel free to get creative with the toppings, using your favorite sushi ingredients. You can also drizzle additional sauce over the top for added flavor. Sushi Pizza is a playful and customizable dish that's perfect for sharing.

Japanese Curry Pizza

Ingredients:

For the Japanese Curry Sauce:

- 2 tablespoons vegetable oil
- 1 onion, finely chopped
- 2 carrots, diced
- 2 potatoes, diced
- 1 pound (450g) boneless chicken thighs or beef, cut into bite-sized pieces
- 3 tablespoons curry powder
- 2 tablespoons all-purpose flour
- 3 cups chicken or vegetable broth
- 2 tablespoons soy sauce
- 1 tablespoon honey or sugar
- Salt and pepper to taste

For the Pizza:

- 1 pizza dough (store-bought or homemade)
- 1 cup shredded mozzarella cheese
- 1 cup cooked Japanese curry sauce (cooled)
- 1 bell pepper, thinly sliced
- 1 cup cooked and shredded chicken or beef (from the curry sauce)
- Fresh cilantro or parsley for garnish

Instructions:

Prepare Japanese Curry Sauce:
- In a large pot, heat vegetable oil over medium heat. Add chopped onions and cook until softened.
- Add diced carrots and potatoes to the pot and cook for a few minutes.
- Add the chicken or beef to the pot and cook until browned.
- Sprinkle curry powder and flour over the ingredients, stirring well to coat.
- Pour in the chicken or vegetable broth, soy sauce, and honey or sugar. Stir until well combined.

- Bring the mixture to a simmer, then reduce heat and let it simmer until the vegetables are tender and the curry sauce thickens. Season with salt and pepper to taste. Set aside to cool.

Preheat Oven:
- Preheat your oven according to the pizza dough package instructions.

Roll Out Pizza Dough:
- Roll out the pizza dough on a floured surface to your desired thickness.

Assemble Pizza:
- Place the rolled-out dough on a pizza stone or baking sheet.
- Spread a layer of shredded mozzarella cheese over the dough.
- Spoon the cooled Japanese curry sauce over the cheese.
- Add thinly sliced bell peppers and the cooked, shredded chicken or beef from the curry sauce.

Bake:
- Follow the pizza dough package instructions for baking. Typically, bake in a preheated oven until the crust is golden, and the cheese is melted and bubbly.

Garnish:
- Garnish the Japanese Curry Pizza with fresh cilantro or parsley.

Serve:
- Slice the pizza into portions and serve hot.

Enjoy the unique and savory taste of Japanese curry in pizza form! Customize with additional toppings or drizzle extra curry sauce for more flavor if desired.

Soba Noodle Pizza

Ingredients:

For the Soba Noodles:

- 200g soba noodles
- 1 tablespoon sesame oil
- 2 tablespoons soy sauce
- 1 tablespoon rice vinegar
- 1 tablespoon mirin
- 1 teaspoon sugar

For the Pizza:

- 1 pizza dough (store-bought or homemade)
- 1 cup shredded mozzarella cheese
- 1/2 cup sliced shiitake mushrooms
- 1/2 cup julienned carrots
- 1/2 cup snow peas, trimmed and sliced
- 1/4 cup sliced green onions
- 1 tablespoon sesame seeds (for garnish)
- 1 tablespoon pickled ginger (for garnish)

Instructions:

Prepare Soba Noodles:
- Cook the soba noodles according to package instructions.
- In a bowl, mix sesame oil, soy sauce, rice vinegar, mirin, and sugar.
- Drain the cooked soba noodles and toss them in the sauce mixture. Set aside to cool.

Preheat Oven:
- Preheat your oven according to the pizza dough package instructions.

Roll Out Pizza Dough:
- Roll out the pizza dough on a floured surface to your desired thickness.

Assemble Pizza:
- Place the rolled-out dough on a pizza stone or baking sheet.

- Evenly spread the marinated soba noodles over the pizza dough.
- Sprinkle shredded mozzarella cheese over the noodles.
- Add sliced shiitake mushrooms, julienned carrots, snow peas, and sliced green onions as toppings.

Bake:
- Follow the pizza dough package instructions for baking. Typically, bake in a preheated oven until the crust is golden, and the cheese is melted and bubbly.

Garnish:
- Sprinkle sesame seeds over the baked pizza for added texture.
- Garnish with pickled ginger for a burst of flavor.

Serve:
- Slice the Soba Noodle Pizza into portions and serve hot.

Enjoy the delightful combination of soba noodles and pizza goodness! This fusion dish offers a unique twist with Asian flavors and is sure to be a hit. Feel free to customize with your favorite vegetables or additional toppings.

Wasabi Mayo Shrimp Pizza

Ingredients:

For the Wasabi Mayo Sauce:

- 3 tablespoons mayonnaise
- 1 teaspoon wasabi paste (adjust to taste)
- 1 teaspoon soy sauce
- 1 teaspoon rice vinegar

For the Pizza:

- 1 pizza dough (store-bought or homemade)
- 1 cup cooked and peeled shrimp, chopped
- 1 cup shredded mozzarella cheese
- 1/2 cup thinly sliced red bell pepper
- 1/2 cup thinly sliced cucumber
- 2 tablespoons sliced green onions
- Sesame seeds for garnish

Instructions:

Preheat Oven:
- Preheat your oven according to the pizza dough package instructions.

Make Wasabi Mayo Sauce:
- In a small bowl, mix together mayonnaise, wasabi paste, soy sauce, and rice vinegar. Adjust the wasabi amount according to your spice preference.

Roll Out Pizza Dough:
- Roll out the pizza dough on a floured surface to your desired thickness.

Assemble Pizza:
- Place the rolled-out dough on a pizza stone or baking sheet.
- Spread the Wasabi Mayo Sauce over the pizza dough, leaving a small border around the edges.
- Sprinkle shredded mozzarella cheese over the sauce.
- Distribute the chopped cooked shrimp, sliced red bell pepper, and sliced cucumber evenly over the pizza.

Bake:

- Follow the pizza dough package instructions for baking. Typically, bake in a preheated oven until the crust is golden, and the cheese is melted and bubbly.

Garnish:
- Sprinkle sliced green onions and sesame seeds over the baked pizza for added flavor and texture.

Serve:
- Slice the Wasabi Mayo Shrimp Pizza into portions and serve hot.

Enjoy the bold and zesty flavors of wasabi mayo paired with succulent shrimp! This unique pizza is sure to tantalize your taste buds. Feel free to customize with additional toppings or drizzle extra wasabi mayo sauce for an extra kick.

Sesame Beef Yakiniku Pizza

Ingredients:

For the Yakiniku Beef:

- 1/2 pound (225g) thinly sliced beef (sirloin or ribeye)
- 2 tablespoons soy sauce
- 1 tablespoon mirin
- 1 tablespoon sake
- 1 tablespoon sugar
- 1 tablespoon sesame oil
- 2 cloves garlic, minced
- 1 teaspoon grated ginger
- 1 tablespoon sesame seeds (for garnish)

For the Pizza:

- 1 pizza dough (store-bought or homemade)
- 1 cup shredded mozzarella cheese
- 1/2 cup sliced red bell pepper
- 1/2 cup sliced green bell pepper
- 1/4 cup sliced red onion
- 2 tablespoons chopped green onions (for garnish)
- 1 tablespoon sesame seeds (for garnish)

Instructions:

Preheat Oven:
- Preheat your oven according to the pizza dough package instructions.

Prepare Yakiniku Beef:
- In a bowl, mix together soy sauce, mirin, sake, sugar, sesame oil, minced garlic, and grated ginger.
- Marinate the thinly sliced beef in the yakiniku sauce for at least 15-20 minutes.

Cook Yakiniku Beef:
- Heat a pan or skillet over medium-high heat.
- Cook the marinated beef slices until browned and cooked through. Set aside.

Roll Out Pizza Dough:

- Roll out the pizza dough on a floured surface to your desired thickness.

Assemble Pizza:
- Place the rolled-out dough on a pizza stone or baking sheet.
- Sprinkle a layer of shredded mozzarella cheese over the dough.
- Distribute the cooked yakiniku beef over the cheese.
- Add sliced red and green bell peppers, and sliced red onion as toppings.

Bake:
- Follow the pizza dough package instructions for baking. Typically, bake in a preheated oven until the crust is golden, and the cheese is melted and bubbly.

Garnish:
- Sprinkle chopped green onions and sesame seeds over the baked pizza for added flavor and texture.

Serve:
- Slice the Sesame Beef Yakiniku Pizza into portions and serve hot.

Enjoy the delightful combination of yakiniku beef, vegetables, and sesame seeds on your pizza! Customize with your favorite toppings or drizzle extra yakiniku sauce for an extra burst of flavor.

Mentaiko and Shiso Pizza

Ingredients:

For the Mentaiko Spread:

- 1/2 cup mentaiko (spicy cod roe)
- 2 tablespoons mayonnaise
- 1 teaspoon soy sauce
- 1 teaspoon mirin (optional)

For the Pizza:

- 1 pizza dough (store-bought or homemade)
- 1 cup shredded mozzarella cheese
- 1/4 cup sliced shiso leaves
- 1/4 cup sliced green onions
- 1 tablespoon sesame seeds
- 1 tablespoon olive oil (for drizzling)

Instructions:

Preheat Oven:
- Preheat your oven according to the pizza dough package instructions.

Prepare Mentaiko Spread:
- In a bowl, mix together mentaiko, mayonnaise, soy sauce, and mirin until well combined. Adjust the quantities according to your taste preference.

Roll Out Pizza Dough:
- Roll out the pizza dough on a floured surface to your desired thickness.

Assemble Pizza:
- Place the rolled-out dough on a pizza stone or baking sheet.
- Spread the mentaiko mixture evenly over the pizza dough, leaving a small border around the edges.
- Sprinkle shredded mozzarella cheese over the mentaiko spread.
- Scatter sliced shiso leaves and green onions over the cheese.

Bake:
- Follow the pizza dough package instructions for baking. Typically, bake in a preheated oven until the crust is golden, and the cheese is melted and bubbly.

Garnish:

- Sprinkle sesame seeds over the baked pizza for added texture.
- Drizzle olive oil over the pizza for an extra layer of richness.

Serve:
- Slice the Mentaiko and Shiso Pizza into portions and serve hot.

Enjoy the unique combination of the creamy mentaiko spread, the freshness of shiso leaves, and the gooey goodness of melted cheese on your pizza! Customize with additional toppings or drizzle extra mentaiko sauce for more flavor.

Matcha Dessert Pizza

Ingredients:

For the Matcha Pizza Dough:

- 1 pizza dough (store-bought or homemade)
- 2 tablespoons matcha powder
- 1/4 cup granulated sugar
- 1/4 cup warm water
- 1 teaspoon vanilla extract
- 2 tablespoons olive oil

For the Matcha Cream Cheese Spread:

- 4 ounces (113g) cream cheese, softened
- 2 tablespoons powdered sugar
- 1 tablespoon matcha powder
- 1 teaspoon vanilla extract

Toppings:

- Sliced strawberries
- Kiwi slices
- Blueberries
- Shredded coconut
- White chocolate chips or chunks
- Mint leaves for garnish

Instructions:

Preheat Oven:
- Preheat your oven according to the pizza dough package instructions.

Prepare Matcha Pizza Dough:
- In a small bowl, whisk together matcha powder, granulated sugar, warm water, vanilla extract, and olive oil until well combined.
- Add the matcha mixture to the pizza dough and knead until evenly distributed.

Roll Out Pizza Dough:

- Roll out the matcha-infused pizza dough on a floured surface to your desired thickness.

Bake:
- Place the rolled-out dough on a pizza stone or baking sheet.
- Follow the pizza dough package instructions for baking. Typically, bake in a preheated oven until the crust is golden.

Prepare Matcha Cream Cheese Spread:
- In a bowl, mix together softened cream cheese, powdered sugar, matcha powder, and vanilla extract until smooth.

Assemble Pizza:
- Once the pizza crust has cooled slightly, spread the matcha cream cheese mixture evenly over the crust.

Add Toppings:
- Decorate the matcha dessert pizza with sliced strawberries, kiwi slices, blueberries, shredded coconut, and white chocolate chips or chunks.

Garnish:
- Garnish the pizza with fresh mint leaves for a burst of color and freshness.

Serve:
- Slice the Matcha Dessert Pizza into portions and serve at room temperature.

Enjoy the delightful combination of matcha-infused crust, sweet cream cheese, and fresh fruit toppings! This dessert pizza is perfect for sharing and makes for a unique and visually appealing treat.

Yuzu Salmon Pizza

Ingredients:

For the Yuzu Salmon:

- 1 pound (450g) salmon fillet, skinless
- 2 tablespoons yuzu juice
- 1 tablespoon soy sauce
- 1 tablespoon honey
- 1 teaspoon grated ginger
- 1 teaspoon sesame oil

For the Pizza:

- 1 pizza dough (store-bought or homemade)
- 1 cup shredded mozzarella cheese
- 1/4 cup thinly sliced red onion
- 1/4 cup thinly sliced cucumber
- 2 tablespoons chopped fresh cilantro
- Sesame seeds for garnish

For the Yuzu Drizzle:

- 2 tablespoons yuzu juice
- 1 tablespoon honey

Instructions:

Preheat Oven:
- Preheat your oven according to the pizza dough package instructions.

Prepare Yuzu Salmon:
- In a bowl, mix together yuzu juice, soy sauce, honey, grated ginger, and sesame oil.
- Place the salmon fillet in a shallow dish and pour the yuzu mixture over it. Marinate for about 15-20 minutes.

Cook Yuzu Salmon:
- Preheat a skillet or grill pan over medium-high heat.

- Cook the marinated salmon for about 3-4 minutes per side, or until cooked to your liking.
- Once cooked, flake the salmon into bite-sized pieces.

Roll Out Pizza Dough:
- Roll out the pizza dough on a floured surface to your desired thickness.

Assemble Pizza:
- Place the rolled-out dough on a pizza stone or baking sheet.
- Sprinkle a layer of shredded mozzarella cheese over the dough.
- Distribute the flaked yuzu salmon over the cheese.
- Add thinly sliced red onion and cucumber as toppings.

Bake:
- Follow the pizza dough package instructions for baking. Typically, bake in a preheated oven until the crust is golden, and the cheese is melted and bubbly.

Yuzu Drizzle:
- In a small bowl, mix together yuzu juice and honey to create a drizzling sauce.

Garnish:
- Drizzle the yuzu mixture over the baked pizza.
- Sprinkle chopped fresh cilantro and sesame seeds over the top for added flavor and texture.

Serve:
- Slice the Yuzu Salmon Pizza into portions and serve hot.

Enjoy the refreshing citrusy kick of yuzu combined with the succulent taste of salmon on your pizza! This fusion dish offers a unique and delightful flavor experience.

Japanese Mushroom Pizza

Ingredients:

For the Sauteed Mushrooms:

- 2 cups mixed mushrooms (shiitake, oyster, enoki, shimeji, etc.), cleaned and sliced
- 2 tablespoons soy sauce
- 1 tablespoon mirin
- 1 tablespoon sake
- 1 tablespoon sesame oil
- 1 teaspoon grated ginger
- 2 cloves garlic, minced

For the Pizza:

- 1 pizza dough (store-bought or homemade)
- 1 cup shredded mozzarella cheese
- 1/4 cup sliced green onions
- 1 tablespoon sesame seeds
- Drizzle of sesame oil (for finishing)

Instructions:

Preheat Oven:
- Preheat your oven according to the pizza dough package instructions.

Prepare Sauteed Mushrooms:
- In a pan, heat sesame oil over medium heat. Add minced garlic and grated ginger, sautéing for about 1 minute until fragrant.
- Add sliced mushrooms to the pan and cook for a few minutes until they start to soften.
- Pour in soy sauce, mirin, and sake. Continue to cook until the mushrooms are tender and the liquid has mostly evaporated. Set aside.

Roll Out Pizza Dough:
- Roll out the pizza dough on a floured surface to your desired thickness.

Assemble Pizza:

- Place the rolled-out dough on a pizza stone or baking sheet.
- Sprinkle a layer of shredded mozzarella cheese over the dough.
- Spread the sauteed mushrooms evenly over the cheese.
- Add sliced green onions as toppings.

Bake:
- Follow the pizza dough package instructions for baking. Typically, bake in a preheated oven until the crust is golden, and the cheese is melted and bubbly.

Garnish:
- Sprinkle sesame seeds over the baked pizza for added texture.
- Drizzle a bit of sesame oil over the top for extra flavor.

Serve:
- Slice the Japanese Mushroom Pizza into portions and serve hot.

Enjoy the rich umami flavors of the assorted mushrooms combined with the nutty essence of sesame on your pizza! Feel free to customize with additional toppings or a sprinkle of your favorite herbs for extra freshness.

Ginger Pork Gyoza Pizza

Ingredients:

For the Ginger Pork:

- 1/2 pound (225g) ground pork
- 2 tablespoons soy sauce
- 1 tablespoon mirin
- 1 tablespoon sake
- 1 tablespoon grated ginger
- 2 cloves garlic, minced
- 1 tablespoon sesame oil

For the Pizza:

- 1 pizza dough (store-bought or homemade)
- 1 cup shredded mozzarella cheese
- 1/2 cup thinly sliced napa cabbage
- 1/4 cup sliced green onions
- Gyoza dumplings (store-bought or homemade), cooked and sliced
- 1 tablespoon sesame seeds (for garnish)
- Drizzle of soy sauce (for finishing)

Instructions:

Preheat Oven:
- Preheat your oven according to the pizza dough package instructions.

Prepare Ginger Pork:
- In a skillet over medium heat, heat sesame oil. Add minced garlic and grated ginger, sautéing for about 1 minute until fragrant.
- Add ground pork to the skillet and cook until browned.
- Pour in soy sauce, mirin, and sake. Continue to cook until the pork is cooked through and the liquid has mostly evaporated. Set aside.

Roll Out Pizza Dough:

- Roll out the pizza dough on a floured surface to your desired thickness.

Assemble Pizza:
- Place the rolled-out dough on a pizza stone or baking sheet.
- Sprinkle a layer of shredded mozzarella cheese over the dough.
- Spread the cooked ginger pork evenly over the cheese.
- Add thinly sliced napa cabbage and sliced gyoza dumplings as toppings.
- Sprinkle sliced green onions over the pizza.

Bake:
- Follow the pizza dough package instructions for baking. Typically, bake in a preheated oven until the crust is golden, and the cheese is melted and bubbly.

Garnish:
- Sprinkle sesame seeds over the baked pizza for added texture.
- Drizzle a bit of soy sauce over the top for extra flavor.

Serve:
- Slice the Ginger Pork Gyoza Pizza into portions and serve hot.

Enjoy the delicious combination of ginger-infused pork, gyoza elements, and the cheesy goodness of pizza! Customize with additional toppings or drizzle extra soy sauce for an extra burst of flavor.

Ginger Pork Gyoza Pizza

Ingredients:

For the Ginger Pork:

- 1/2 pound (225g) ground pork
- 2 tablespoons soy sauce
- 1 tablespoon mirin
- 1 tablespoon sake
- 1 tablespoon grated ginger
- 2 cloves garlic, minced
- 1 tablespoon sesame oil

For the Pizza:

- 1 pizza dough (store-bought or homemade)
- 1 cup shredded mozzarella cheese
- 1/2 cup thinly sliced napa cabbage
- 1/4 cup sliced green onions
- Gyoza dumplings (store-bought or homemade), cooked and sliced
- 1 tablespoon sesame seeds (for garnish)
- Drizzle of soy sauce (for finishing)

Instructions:

Preheat Oven:
- Preheat your oven according to the pizza dough package instructions.

Prepare Ginger Pork:
- In a skillet over medium heat, heat sesame oil. Add minced garlic and grated ginger, sautéing for about 1 minute until fragrant.
- Add ground pork to the skillet and cook until browned.
- Pour in soy sauce, mirin, and sake. Continue to cook until the pork is cooked through and the liquid has mostly evaporated. Set aside.

Roll Out Pizza Dough:

- Roll out the pizza dough on a floured surface to your desired thickness.

Assemble Pizza:
- Place the rolled-out dough on a pizza stone or baking sheet.
- Sprinkle a layer of shredded mozzarella cheese over the dough.
- Spread the cooked ginger pork evenly over the cheese.
- Add thinly sliced napa cabbage and sliced gyoza dumplings as toppings.
- Sprinkle sliced green onions over the pizza.

Bake:
- Follow the pizza dough package instructions for baking. Typically, bake in a preheated oven until the crust is golden, and the cheese is melted and bubbly.

Garnish:
- Sprinkle sesame seeds over the baked pizza for added texture.
- Drizzle a bit of soy sauce over the top for extra flavor.

Serve:
- Slice the Ginger Pork Gyoza Pizza into portions and serve hot.

Enjoy the delicious combination of ginger-infused pork, gyoza elements, and the cheesy goodness of pizza! Customize with additional toppings or drizzle extra soy sauce for an extra burst of flavor.

Edamame and Avocado Pizza

Ingredients:

For the Pizza:

- 1 pizza dough (store-bought or homemade)
- 1 cup shredded mozzarella cheese
- 1 cup cooked edamame, shelled
- 1 ripe avocado, sliced
- 1/4 cup sliced red onion
- 1/4 cup crumbled feta cheese (optional)
- 2 tablespoons chopped fresh cilantro
- Olive oil for drizzling
- Red pepper flakes for a hint of heat (optional)
- Salt and pepper to taste

Instructions:

Preheat Oven:
- Preheat your oven according to the pizza dough package instructions.

Roll Out Pizza Dough:
- Roll out the pizza dough on a floured surface to your desired thickness.

Assemble Pizza:
- Place the rolled-out dough on a pizza stone or baking sheet.
- Sprinkle a layer of shredded mozzarella cheese over the dough.
- Evenly distribute the cooked edamame, sliced avocado, and sliced red onion as toppings.
- If using, sprinkle crumbled feta cheese over the pizza.

Season and Drizzle:
- Season the pizza with salt and pepper to taste.
- Drizzle olive oil over the top for added richness.

Bake:

- Follow the pizza dough package instructions for baking. Typically, bake in a preheated oven until the crust is golden, and the cheese is melted and bubbly.

Garnish:
- Sprinkle chopped fresh cilantro over the baked pizza.
- If you like a bit of heat, you can add red pepper flakes for a spicy kick.

Serve:
- Slice the Edamame and Avocado Pizza into portions and serve hot.

Enjoy the delightful combination of creamy avocado, nutty edamame, and the cheesy goodness of pizza! This pizza is not only delicious but also packed with vibrant colors and healthy ingredients. Feel free to customize with additional toppings or a drizzle of your favorite sauce.

Wakame Seaweed Pizza

Ingredients:

For the Pizza:

- 1 pizza dough (store-bought or homemade)
- 1 cup shredded mozzarella cheese
- 1/2 cup wakame seaweed, rehydrated and chopped
- 1/4 cup sliced black olives
- 1/4 cup sliced red bell pepper
- 1/4 cup sliced green onions
- 2 tablespoons sesame seeds
- Soy sauce for drizzling

For the Sauce:

- 3 tablespoons mayonnaise
- 1 tablespoon soy sauce
- 1 teaspoon rice vinegar
- 1 teaspoon honey or sugar

Instructions:

Preheat Oven:
- Preheat your oven according to the pizza dough package instructions.

Rehydrate Wakame Seaweed:
- Soak the wakame seaweed in warm water for about 5 minutes or until it's rehydrated. Drain and chop.

Roll Out Pizza Dough:
- Roll out the pizza dough on a floured surface to your desired thickness.

Prepare Sauce:

- In a small bowl, mix together mayonnaise, soy sauce, rice vinegar, and honey (or sugar) to create the sauce.

Assemble Pizza:
- Place the rolled-out dough on a pizza stone or baking sheet.
- Spread the sauce evenly over the dough, leaving a small border around the edges.
- Sprinkle shredded mozzarella cheese over the sauce.
- Distribute rehydrated and chopped wakame seaweed, sliced black olives, sliced red bell pepper, and sliced green onions as toppings.

Bake:
- Follow the pizza dough package instructions for baking. Typically, bake in a preheated oven until the crust is golden, and the cheese is melted and bubbly.

Garnish:
- Sprinkle sesame seeds over the baked pizza for added texture.
- Drizzle soy sauce over the top for an extra burst of umami.

Serve:
- Slice the Wakame Seaweed Pizza into portions and serve hot.

Enjoy the distinctive flavor of wakame seaweed combined with the savory elements of pizza! This fusion dish offers a unique twist and is sure to be a conversation starter.

Feel free to customize with additional toppings or adjust the sauce to your taste.

Yakitori Chicken Skewer Pizza

Ingredients:

For the Yakitori Chicken Skewers:

- 1 pound (450g) boneless, skinless chicken thighs, cut into bite-sized pieces
- 1/4 cup soy sauce
- 2 tablespoons sake
- 2 tablespoons mirin
- 1 tablespoon honey or sugar
- 1 clove garlic, minced
- 1 teaspoon grated ginger
- Bamboo skewers, soaked in water for at least 30 minutes

For the Pizza:

- 1 pizza dough (store-bought or homemade)
- 1 cup shredded mozzarella cheese
- 1/2 cup thinly sliced green onions
- 1/4 cup yakitori sauce (reserved from marinating)
- 1 tablespoon sesame seeds
- Shichimi togarashi (Japanese seven spice) for extra flavor (optional)

Instructions:

Marinate Chicken:
- In a bowl, combine soy sauce, sake, mirin, honey (or sugar), minced garlic, and grated ginger. Set aside a portion (about 1/4 cup) for the pizza sauce.
- Marinate the chicken pieces in the remaining sauce for at least 30 minutes, or ideally, refrigerate for a few hours for more flavor.

Prepare Yakitori Chicken Skewers:
- Preheat your grill or grill pan.
- Thread the marinated chicken pieces onto the soaked bamboo skewers.
- Grill the skewers until the chicken is cooked through and has a nice char, basting with the marinade.

Preheat Oven:
- Preheat your oven according to the pizza dough package instructions.

Roll Out Pizza Dough:
- Roll out the pizza dough on a floured surface to your desired thickness.

Assemble Pizza:
- Place the rolled-out dough on a pizza stone or baking sheet.
- Spread a layer of shredded mozzarella cheese over the dough.
- Distribute the cooked yakitori chicken pieces, thinly sliced green onions, and sesame seeds evenly over the cheese.
- Drizzle the reserved yakitori sauce over the top.

Bake:
- Follow the pizza dough package instructions for baking. Typically, bake in a preheated oven until the crust is golden, and the cheese is melted and bubbly.

Garnish:
- Sprinkle shichimi togarashi over the baked pizza for an extra kick (optional).

Serve:
- Slice the Yakitori Chicken Skewer Pizza into portions and serve hot.

Enjoy the savory and slightly sweet flavors of yakitori chicken on a pizza crust! This fusion dish is a delightful combination of Japanese and Italian cuisines. Customize with additional toppings or drizzle extra sauce for more flavor if desired.

Japanese Plum (Ume) Pizza

Ingredients:

For the Ume Sauce:

- 1/2 cup ume paste (available in Japanese or Asian grocery stores)
- 2 tablespoons honey
- 1 tablespoon rice vinegar
- 1 tablespoon soy sauce

For the Pizza:

- 1 pizza dough (store-bought or homemade)
- 1 cup shredded mozzarella cheese
- 1/4 cup sliced shiitake mushrooms
- 1/4 cup crumbled tofu or diced firm tofu
- 1/4 cup sliced green onions
- 1 tablespoon sesame seeds
- Shiso leaves for garnish (optional)

Instructions:

Preheat Oven:
- Preheat your oven according to the pizza dough package instructions.

Prepare Ume Sauce:
- In a bowl, mix together ume paste, honey, rice vinegar, and soy sauce to create the ume sauce. Adjust the sweetness and tartness according to your taste.

Roll Out Pizza Dough:
- Roll out the pizza dough on a floured surface to your desired thickness.

Assemble Pizza:
- Place the rolled-out dough on a pizza stone or baking sheet.
- Spread a layer of ume sauce evenly over the dough, leaving a small border around the edges.
- Sprinkle shredded mozzarella cheese over the ume sauce.
- Add sliced shiitake mushrooms, crumbled tofu or diced firm tofu, and sliced green onions as toppings.

Bake:
- Follow the pizza dough package instructions for baking. Typically, bake in a preheated oven until the crust is golden, and the cheese is melted and bubbly.

Garnish:
- Sprinkle sesame seeds over the baked pizza for added texture.
- If available, garnish with fresh shiso leaves for an extra layer of flavor.

Serve:
- Slice the Japanese Plum (Ume) Pizza into portions and serve hot.

Enjoy the unique and vibrant taste of Japanese plum on your pizza! This fusion dish offers a sweet and tart flavor profile with a touch of umami. Feel free to customize with additional toppings or drizzle extra ume sauce for more intensity.

Sesame-Crusted Tofu Pizza

Ingredients:

For the Sesame-Crusted Tofu:

- 1 block extra-firm tofu, pressed and sliced into 1/2-inch cubes
- 2 tablespoons soy sauce
- 1 tablespoon sesame oil
- 1 tablespoon rice vinegar
- 1 tablespoon maple syrup or agave nectar
- 2 tablespoons sesame seeds
- 1 tablespoon cornstarch
- Cooking oil for frying

For the Pizza:

- 1 pizza dough (store-bought or homemade)
- 1 cup shredded vegan mozzarella cheese
- 1/2 cup sliced bell peppers (assorted colors)
- 1/4 cup sliced red onion
- 1/4 cup sliced black olives
- 2 tablespoons chopped fresh cilantro or parsley
- 1 tablespoon sesame seeds for garnish
- Sriracha or your favorite hot sauce for drizzling (optional)

Instructions:

Preheat Oven:
- Preheat your oven according to the pizza dough package instructions.

Prepare Sesame-Crusted Tofu:
- In a bowl, whisk together soy sauce, sesame oil, rice vinegar, and maple syrup (or agave nectar).

- Toss the tofu cubes in the marinade and let them marinate for at least 15-20 minutes.
- In a separate bowl, mix sesame seeds and cornstarch.
- Roll the marinated tofu cubes in the sesame seed mixture, ensuring they are well-coated.
- In a skillet, heat cooking oil over medium heat. Fry the sesame-crusted tofu cubes until golden brown on all sides. Remove from heat and set aside.

Roll Out Pizza Dough:
- Roll out the pizza dough on a floured surface to your desired thickness.

Assemble Pizza:
- Place the rolled-out dough on a pizza stone or baking sheet.
- Sprinkle a layer of shredded vegan mozzarella cheese over the dough.
- Distribute the fried sesame-crusted tofu cubes, sliced bell peppers, sliced red onion, and black olives evenly over the cheese.

Bake:
- Follow the pizza dough package instructions for baking. Typically, bake in a preheated oven until the crust is golden, and the cheese is melted and bubbly.

Garnish:
- Sprinkle sesame seeds over the baked pizza for added texture.
- Garnish with chopped fresh cilantro or parsley.

Serve:
- Drizzle with sriracha or your favorite hot sauce if you like it spicy.
- Slice the Sesame-Crusted Tofu Pizza into portions and serve hot.

Enjoy the nutty crunch of sesame-crusted tofu combined with colorful veggies on your pizza! This plant-based option is not only delicious but also packed with protein and flavor. Customize with additional toppings or sauces to suit your taste.

Nikujaga Beef Pizza

Ingredients:

For the Nikujaga Beef:

- 1/2 pound (225g) thinly sliced beef (such as ribeye or sirloin)
- 2 potatoes, peeled and thinly sliced
- 1 onion, thinly sliced
- 1 carrot, thinly sliced
- 1 cup green beans, cut into bite-sized pieces
- 2 tablespoons vegetable oil
- 1/4 cup soy sauce
- 1/4 cup mirin
- 2 tablespoons sake
- 2 tablespoons sugar
- 1 cup dashi broth (or substitute with beef or vegetable broth)

For the Pizza:

- 1 pizza dough (store-bought or homemade)
- 1 cup shredded mozzarella cheese
- 1/4 cup sliced green onions
- 1 tablespoon sesame seeds (for garnish)
- Shichimi togarashi (Japanese seven spice) for added spice (optional)

Instructions:

Preheat Oven:
- Preheat your oven according to the pizza dough package instructions.

Prepare Nikujaga Beef:
- In a large pan or skillet, heat vegetable oil over medium heat.

- Add thinly sliced beef and cook until browned. Remove excess oil if needed.
- Add sliced potatoes, onion, carrot, and green beans to the pan.
- In a bowl, mix together soy sauce, mirin, sake, sugar, and dashi broth. Pour the mixture over the ingredients in the pan.
- Simmer until the vegetables are tender and the liquid has reduced to a flavorful sauce.

Roll Out Pizza Dough:
- Roll out the pizza dough on a floured surface to your desired thickness.

Assemble Pizza:
- Place the rolled-out dough on a pizza stone or baking sheet.
- Spread a layer of shredded mozzarella cheese over the dough.
- Distribute the cooked Nikujaga Beef (meat and vegetables) evenly over the cheese.

Bake:
- Follow the pizza dough package instructions for baking. Typically, bake in a preheated oven until the crust is golden, and the cheese is melted and bubbly.

Garnish:
- Sprinkle sliced green onions, sesame seeds, and shichimi togarashi (if using) over the baked pizza for added flavor and texture.

Serve:
- Slice the Nikujaga Beef Pizza into portions and serve hot.

Enjoy the comforting flavors of Nikujaga Beef on a pizza crust! This fusion dish offers a unique twist with the savory beef and vegetable stew topping. Customize with additional toppings or add extra spice for a flavorful kick.

Soy-Glazed Shitake Pizza

Ingredients:

For the Soy-Glazed Shiitake Mushrooms:

- 2 cups shiitake mushrooms, stems removed and sliced
- 2 tablespoons soy sauce
- 1 tablespoon mirin
- 1 tablespoon sesame oil
- 1 tablespoon brown sugar
- 1 teaspoon grated ginger
- 2 cloves garlic, minced

For the Pizza:

- 1 pizza dough (store-bought or homemade)
- 1 cup shredded mozzarella cheese
- 1/4 cup sliced red bell pepper
- 1/4 cup sliced green onions
- 1 tablespoon sesame seeds
- Drizzle of extra soy sauce for finishing

Instructions:

Preheat Oven:
- Preheat your oven according to the pizza dough package instructions.

Prepare Soy-Glazed Shiitake Mushrooms:
- In a bowl, whisk together soy sauce, mirin, sesame oil, brown sugar, grated ginger, and minced garlic.

- Add sliced shiitake mushrooms to the bowl, ensuring they are well-coated in the marinade. Let them marinate for at least 15-20 minutes.

Roll Out Pizza Dough:
- Roll out the pizza dough on a floured surface to your desired thickness.

Assemble Pizza:
- Place the rolled-out dough on a pizza stone or baking sheet.
- Sprinkle a layer of shredded mozzarella cheese over the dough.
- Distribute the marinated shiitake mushrooms evenly over the cheese.
- Add sliced red bell pepper and green onions as additional toppings.

Bake:
- Follow the pizza dough package instructions for baking. Typically, bake in a preheated oven until the crust is golden, and the cheese is melted and bubbly.

Garnish:
- Sprinkle sesame seeds over the baked pizza for added texture.
- Drizzle extra soy sauce over the top for an additional burst of flavor.

Serve:
- Slice the Soy-Glazed Shiitake Pizza into portions and serve hot.

Enjoy the savory and slightly sweet flavors of soy-glazed shiitake mushrooms combined with the cheesy goodness of pizza! This fusion dish is a delightful combination of Asian and Italian cuisines. Customize with additional toppings or drizzle extra soy sauce for an extra layer of umami.

Sakura Cherry Blossom Pizza

Ingredients:

For the Cherry Blossom Sauce:

- 1/2 cup mascarpone cheese
- 2 tablespoons honey
- 1 teaspoon cherry blossom extract or cherry blossom syrup (available in Japanese or specialty stores)
- 1/4 teaspoon almond extract (optional)

For the Pizza:

- 1 pizza dough (store-bought or homemade)
- 1 cup fresh mozzarella cheese, torn into small pieces
- 1/2 cup prosciutto, thinly sliced
- 1/4 cup cherry tomatoes, halved
- 1/4 cup arugula, for garnish
- Edible flowers for decoration (optional)
- 1 tablespoon sesame seeds (black or white), for garnish

Instructions:

Preheat Oven:
- Preheat your oven according to the pizza dough package instructions.

Prepare Cherry Blossom Sauce:
- In a bowl, combine mascarpone cheese, honey, cherry blossom extract or syrup, and almond extract. Mix until well combined. Adjust sweetness and flavor to your liking.

Roll Out Pizza Dough:

- Roll out the pizza dough on a floured surface to your desired thickness.

Assemble Pizza:
- Place the rolled-out dough on a pizza stone or baking sheet.
- Spread a layer of the cherry blossom sauce over the dough, leaving a small border around the edges.
- Sprinkle torn mozzarella cheese over the sauce.
- Add thinly sliced prosciutto and cherry tomato halves as toppings.

Bake:
- Follow the pizza dough package instructions for baking. Typically, bake in a preheated oven until the crust is golden, and the cheese is melted and bubbly.

Garnish:
- Once the pizza is out of the oven, garnish with fresh arugula, edible flowers (if using), and sesame seeds.

Serve:
- Slice the Sakura Cherry Blossom Pizza into portions and serve hot.

Enjoy the unique and floral flavors of cherry blossoms on your pizza! This creative fusion dish is not only visually stunning but also captures the essence of cherry blossoms in both taste and presentation. Feel free to customize with additional toppings or experiment with different edible flowers.

Mochi and Red Bean Pizza

Ingredients:

For the Pizza:

- 1 pizza dough (store-bought or homemade)
- 1 cup sweet red bean paste (anko)
- 1 cup mochi pieces (store-bought or homemade)
- 1/2 cup sliced strawberries
- 1/4 cup crushed kinako (roasted soybean flour)
- 1 tablespoon black sesame seeds, for garnish
- Powdered sugar, for dusting (optional)

For the Mochi:

- 1 cup glutinous rice flour (mochiko)
- 1/4 cup sugar
- 2/3 cup water
- Cornstarch for dusting

Instructions:

For the Mochi:

Prepare Mochi Dough:
- In a heatproof bowl, mix glutinous rice flour and sugar.
- Gradually add water, stirring to create a smooth batter.
- Cover the bowl with plastic wrap and microwave for 2-3 minutes until the mochi mixture becomes thick and sticky.
- Allow the mochi to cool.

Form Mochi Pieces:
- Dust your hands and a clean surface with cornstarch.

- Scoop out portions of the mochi mixture and roll them into small, bite-sized pieces. Dust with more cornstarch to prevent sticking.

For the Pizza:

Preheat Oven:
- Preheat your oven according to the pizza dough package instructions.

Roll Out Pizza Dough:
- Roll out the pizza dough on a floured surface to your desired thickness.

Assemble Pizza:
- Place the rolled-out dough on a pizza stone or baking sheet.
- Spread a layer of sweet red bean paste (anko) over the dough.
- Scatter the mochi pieces evenly on top of the red bean paste.
- Add sliced strawberries as additional toppings.
- Sprinkle crushed kinako over the pizza.

Bake:
- Follow the pizza dough package instructions for baking. Typically, bake in a preheated oven until the crust is golden.

Garnish:
- Sprinkle black sesame seeds over the baked pizza for added texture.
- Optionally, dust the pizza with powdered sugar for extra sweetness.

Serve:
- Slice the Mochi and Red Bean Pizza into portions and serve warm.

Enjoy the delightful combination of chewy mochi, sweet red bean paste, and fresh strawberries on your dessert pizza! This unique fusion dish brings together Japanese and Italian flavors in a sweet and satisfying way.

Yuzu Kosho Shrimp Pizza

Ingredients:

For the Yuzu Kosho Shrimp:

- 1 pound (450g) large shrimp, peeled and deveined
- 2 tablespoons yuzu kosho paste (available in Japanese or specialty stores)
- 2 tablespoons soy sauce
- 1 tablespoon mirin
- 1 tablespoon sesame oil
- 1 tablespoon honey or maple syrup
- 2 cloves garlic, minced
- 1 tablespoon grated ginger

For the Pizza:

- 1 pizza dough (store-bought or homemade)
- 1 cup shredded mozzarella cheese
- 1/2 cup sliced shiitake mushrooms
- 1/4 cup sliced red bell pepper
- 1/4 cup sliced green onions
- Sesame seeds for garnish
- Fresh cilantro or parsley for garnish

Instructions:

For the Yuzu Kosho Shrimp:

Marinate Shrimp:
- In a bowl, combine yuzu kosho paste, soy sauce, mirin, sesame oil, honey (or maple syrup), minced garlic, and grated ginger.

- Add the peeled and deveined shrimp to the marinade, ensuring they are well-coated. Marinate for at least 15-20 minutes.

Cook Shrimp:
- In a skillet over medium-high heat, cook the marinated shrimp until they are opaque and cooked through. Set aside.

For the Pizza:

Preheat Oven:
- Preheat your oven according to the pizza dough package instructions.

Roll Out Pizza Dough:
- Roll out the pizza dough on a floured surface to your desired thickness.

Assemble Pizza:
- Place the rolled-out dough on a pizza stone or baking sheet.
- Sprinkle a layer of shredded mozzarella cheese over the dough.
- Distribute the cooked yuzu kosho shrimp evenly over the cheese.
- Add sliced shiitake mushrooms, sliced red bell pepper, and sliced green onions as additional toppings.

Bake:
- Follow the pizza dough package instructions for baking. Typically, bake in a preheated oven until the crust is golden, and the cheese is melted and bubbly.

Garnish:
- Sprinkle sesame seeds over the baked pizza for added texture.
- Garnish with fresh cilantro or parsley.

Serve:
- Slice the Yuzu Kosho Shrimp Pizza into portions and serve hot.

Enjoy the bold and citrusy flavors of yuzu kosho combined with the succulent shrimp on your pizza! This fusion dish offers a unique and zesty twist that is sure to delight your taste buds. Customize with additional toppings or drizzle extra yuzu kosho for an extra kick.

Shabu-Shabu Beef Pizza

Ingredients:

For the Shabu-Shabu Beef:

- 1/2 pound (225g) thinly sliced beef (such as ribeye or sirloin)
- 2 tablespoons soy sauce
- 1 tablespoon mirin
- 1 tablespoon sake
- 1 tablespoon sugar
- 1 teaspoon sesame oil

For the Pizza:

- 1 pizza dough (store-bought or homemade)
- 1 cup shredded mozzarella cheese
- 1/2 cup shiitake mushrooms, sliced
- 1/4 cup enoki mushrooms, separated
- 1/4 cup sliced green onions
- 1 tablespoon sesame seeds
- Ponzu sauce for drizzling
- Shichimi togarashi (Japanese seven spice) for extra flavor (optional)

Instructions:

For the Shabu-Shabu Beef:

    Marinate Beef:
- In a bowl, combine soy sauce, mirin, sake, sugar, and sesame oil.
- Add thinly sliced beef to the marinade, ensuring it is well-coated. Marinate for at least 15-20 minutes.

    Cook Beef:

- In a hot pan or skillet, quickly cook the marinated beef slices until they are just browned. The cooking process should be brief as the beef will continue to cook on the pizza.

For the Pizza:

Preheat Oven:
- Preheat your oven according to the pizza dough package instructions.

Roll Out Pizza Dough:
- Roll out the pizza dough on a floured surface to your desired thickness.

Assemble Pizza:
- Place the rolled-out dough on a pizza stone or baking sheet.
- Sprinkle a layer of shredded mozzarella cheese over the dough.
- Distribute the cooked shabu-shabu beef evenly over the cheese.
- Add sliced shiitake mushrooms, enoki mushrooms, and sliced green onions as additional toppings.

Bake:
- Follow the pizza dough package instructions for baking. Typically, bake in a preheated oven until the crust is golden, and the cheese is melted and bubbly.

Garnish:
- Sprinkle sesame seeds over the baked pizza for added texture.
- Drizzle ponzu sauce over the top for a burst of citrusy flavor.
- Optionally, sprinkle shichimi togarashi for an extra kick.

Serve:
- Slice the Shabu-Shabu Beef Pizza into portions and serve hot.

Enjoy the delicious combination of shabu-shabu beef, mushrooms, and cheese on your pizza! This fusion dish is a delightful blend of Japanese and Italian flavors. Customize with additional toppings or adjust the drizzle for your taste preferences.

Tempura Veggie Pizza

Ingredients:

For the Tempura Batter:

- 1 cup all-purpose flour
- 1 cup ice-cold water
- 1 egg, beaten
- 1/2 teaspoon baking powder
- Ice cubes

For the Tempura Vegetables:

- Assorted vegetables (zucchini, sweet potato, bell peppers, broccoli, etc.), sliced into bite-sized pieces
- Vegetable oil for frying

For the Pizza:

- 1 pizza dough (store-bought or homemade)
- 1 cup shredded mozzarella cheese
- Tempura vegetables (from above)
- 1/4 cup sliced green onions
- Tempura dipping sauce or soy sauce for drizzling
- Sesame seeds for garnish

Instructions:

For the Tempura Batter and Vegetables:

    Prepare Tempura Batter:
- In a bowl, combine all-purpose flour, ice-cold water, beaten egg, and baking powder. Mix until just combined. It's okay if there are lumps.

- Place ice cubes in the batter to keep it cold.

Heat Oil:
- Heat vegetable oil in a deep fryer or a deep, heavy-bottomed pan to 350°F (175°C).

Dip and Fry Vegetables:
- Dip the sliced vegetables into the tempura batter, ensuring they are well-coated.
- Carefully place the battered vegetables into the hot oil and fry until golden brown and crispy. Work in batches to avoid overcrowding the pan.
- Remove the fried vegetables with a slotted spoon and place them on a paper towel-lined plate to drain excess oil.

For the Pizza:

Preheat Oven:
- Preheat your oven according to the pizza dough package instructions.

Roll Out Pizza Dough:
- Roll out the pizza dough on a floured surface to your desired thickness.

Assemble Pizza:
- Place the rolled-out dough on a pizza stone or baking sheet.
- Sprinkle a layer of shredded mozzarella cheese over the dough.
- Distribute the tempura vegetables evenly over the cheese.
- Add sliced green onions as an additional topping.

Bake:
- Follow the pizza dough package instructions for baking. Typically, bake in a preheated oven until the crust is golden, and the cheese is melted and bubbly.

Garnish:
- Drizzle tempura dipping sauce or soy sauce over the baked pizza.
- Sprinkle sesame seeds over the top for added flavor.

Serve:
- Slice the Tempura Veggie Pizza into portions and serve hot.

Enjoy the delightful combination of crispy tempura vegetables and cheesy pizza! This fusion dish offers a satisfying texture contrast and a burst of flavors. Customize with your favorite vegetables and dipping sauce.

Soy-Glazed Black Cod Pizza

Ingredients:

For the Soy-Glazed Black Cod:

- 1 pound (450g) black cod fillets, skin removed
- 3 tablespoons soy sauce
- 2 tablespoons mirin
- 1 tablespoon sake
- 1 tablespoon brown sugar
- 1 tablespoon sesame oil
- 2 cloves garlic, minced
- 1 tablespoon grated ginger
- Sesame seeds for garnish

For the Pizza:

- 1 pizza dough (store-bought or homemade)
- 1 cup shredded mozzarella cheese
- 1/2 cup sliced shiitake mushrooms
- 1/4 cup sliced red bell pepper
- 1/4 cup sliced green onions
- Fresh cilantro for garnish

Instructions:

For the Soy-Glazed Black Cod:

Prepare the Soy Glaze:
- In a bowl, whisk together soy sauce, mirin, sake, brown sugar, sesame oil, minced garlic, and grated ginger to create the soy glaze.

Marinate the Black Cod:
- Place black cod fillets in a shallow dish and pour the soy glaze over them, ensuring they are well-coated.

- Marinate the black cod in the refrigerator for at least 30 minutes.

Cook the Black Cod:
- Preheat your oven to 400°F (200°C).
- Heat a non-stick skillet over medium-high heat.
- Cook the marinated black cod fillets for 2-3 minutes on each side until they are caramelized and cooked through.
- Flake the black cod into bite-sized pieces.

For the Pizza:

Preheat Oven:
- Preheat your oven according to the pizza dough package instructions.

Roll Out Pizza Dough:
- Roll out the pizza dough on a floured surface to your desired thickness.

Assemble Pizza:
- Place the rolled-out dough on a pizza stone or baking sheet.
- Sprinkle a layer of shredded mozzarella cheese over the dough.
- Distribute the flaked soy-glazed black cod evenly over the cheese.
- Add sliced shiitake mushrooms, sliced red bell pepper, and sliced green onions as additional toppings.

Bake:
- Follow the pizza dough package instructions for baking. Typically, bake in a preheated oven until the crust is golden, and the cheese is melted and bubbly.

Garnish:
- Sprinkle sesame seeds over the baked pizza for added texture.
- Garnish with fresh cilantro.

Serve:
- Slice the Soy-Glazed Black Cod Pizza into portions and serve hot.

Enjoy the luxurious and savory flavor of soy-glazed black cod on your pizza! This fusion dish offers a delightful combination of Asian and Italian influences. Customize with additional toppings or drizzle extra soy glaze for an extra burst of flavor.

Tamago (Japanese Omelette) Pizza

Ingredients:

For the Tamago (Japanese Omelette):

- 4 large eggs
- 2 tablespoons sugar
- 1 tablespoon soy sauce
- 1 tablespoon mirin
- 1/2 teaspoon salt
- 1 tablespoon vegetable oil

For the Pizza:

- 1 pizza dough (store-bought or homemade)
- 1 cup shredded mozzarella cheese
- 1/4 cup sliced scallions (green onions)
- 1/4 cup sliced red bell pepper
- 1/4 cup sliced shiitake mushrooms
- 1 tablespoon sesame seeds for garnish
- Drizzle of soy sauce for finishing

Instructions:

For the Tamago (Japanese Omelette):

    Prepare Tamago Mixture:
- In a bowl, whisk together eggs, sugar, soy sauce, mirin, and salt until well combined.

    Cook Tamago:

- Heat a non-stick frying pan over medium heat and add vegetable oil.
- Pour a thin layer of the tamago mixture into the pan, swirling to coat the bottom.
- Cook until the edges start to set, then roll the omelette from one side to the other, creating a log.
- Push the rolled omelette to the side and add more tamago mixture to the empty side of the pan.
- Lift the rolled omelette and let the new mixture flow underneath.
- Repeat the rolling process until all the mixture is used.
- Once cooked, let the tamago log cool and slice it into thin strips.

For the Pizza:

Preheat Oven:
- Preheat your oven according to the pizza dough package instructions.

Roll Out Pizza Dough:
- Roll out the pizza dough on a floured surface to your desired thickness.

Assemble Pizza:
- Place the rolled-out dough on a pizza stone or baking sheet.
- Sprinkle a layer of shredded mozzarella cheese over the dough.
- Distribute the sliced tamago strips, sliced scallions, sliced red bell pepper, and sliced shiitake mushrooms evenly over the cheese.

Bake:
- Follow the pizza dough package instructions for baking. Typically, bake in a preheated oven until the crust is golden, and the cheese is melted and bubbly.

Garnish:
- Sprinkle sesame seeds over the baked pizza for added texture.
- Drizzle soy sauce over the top for an extra burst of flavor.

Serve:
- Slice the Tamago Pizza into portions and serve hot.

Enjoy the delicious combination of sweet and savory tamago with the cheesy goodness of pizza! This fusion dish offers a unique twist on traditional flavors. Customize with additional toppings or add your favorite sauce for extra flavor if desired.

Mushroom Miso Butter Pizza

Ingredients:

For the Miso Butter Sauce:

- 2 tablespoons unsalted butter, softened
- 2 tablespoons white miso paste
- 1 tablespoon honey or maple syrup
- 1 teaspoon soy sauce

For the Pizza:

- 1 pizza dough (store-bought or homemade)
- 1 cup shredded mozzarella cheese
- 1 cup mixed mushrooms (shiitake, cremini, oyster, etc.), sliced
- 1/4 cup sliced red onion
- 2 tablespoons chopped fresh parsley
- Sesame seeds for garnish (optional)

Instructions:

For the Miso Butter Sauce:

    Prepare Miso Butter Sauce:

- In a small bowl, mix together softened butter, white miso paste, honey (or maple syrup), and soy sauce until well combined. Adjust sweetness and saltiness to your liking.

For the Pizza:

Preheat Oven:
- Preheat your oven according to the pizza dough package instructions.

Roll Out Pizza Dough:
- Roll out the pizza dough on a floured surface to your desired thickness.

Assemble Pizza:
- Place the rolled-out dough on a pizza stone or baking sheet.
- Spread a layer of the miso butter sauce evenly over the dough, leaving a small border around the edges.
- Sprinkle a layer of shredded mozzarella cheese over the miso butter sauce.
- Distribute the sliced mixed mushrooms and sliced red onion evenly over the cheese.

Bake:
- Follow the pizza dough package instructions for baking. Typically, bake in a preheated oven until the crust is golden, and the cheese is melted and bubbly.

Garnish:
- Sprinkle chopped fresh parsley over the baked pizza for added freshness.
- Optionally, sprinkle sesame seeds over the top for an extra layer of flavor and texture.

Serve:
- Slice the Mushroom Miso Butter Pizza into portions and serve hot.

Enjoy the rich and savory combination of miso butter and assorted mushrooms on your pizza! This fusion dish offers a unique blend of Japanese and Italian flavors. Customize with additional toppings or drizzle extra miso butter for an extra umami kick.

Yakitori Quail Egg Pizza

Ingredients:

For the Yakitori Chicken:

- 1 cup boneless, skinless chicken thighs, cut into bite-sized pieces
- 2 tablespoons soy sauce
- 1 tablespoon sake
- 1 tablespoon mirin
- 1 tablespoon honey or maple syrup
- 1 clove garlic, minced
- 1 teaspoon grated ginger
- Wooden skewers, soaked in water

For the Pizza:

- 1 pizza dough (store-bought or homemade)
- 1 cup shredded mozzarella cheese
- 8-10 quail eggs, boiled and peeled
- 1/4 cup sliced green onions

- Yakitori chicken (from above)
- 1 tablespoon sesame seeds
- Teriyaki sauce for drizzling (optional)

Instructions:

For the Yakitori Chicken:

Prepare Yakitori Marinade:
- In a bowl, mix together soy sauce, sake, mirin, honey (or maple syrup), minced garlic, and grated ginger to create the yakitori marinade.

Marinate Chicken:
- Place the chicken pieces in the marinade, ensuring they are well-coated. Marinate for at least 30 minutes, or longer for more flavor.

Skewer and Grill:
- Thread the marinated chicken pieces onto soaked wooden skewers.
- Grill the yakitori chicken skewers on a barbecue or grill pan until cooked through and slightly charred.

For the Pizza:

Preheat Oven:
- Preheat your oven according to the pizza dough package instructions.

Roll Out Pizza Dough:
- Roll out the pizza dough on a floured surface to your desired thickness.

Assemble Pizza:
- Place the rolled-out dough on a pizza stone or baking sheet.
- Sprinkle a layer of shredded mozzarella cheese over the dough.
- Distribute the quail eggs, sliced green onions, and grilled yakitori chicken evenly over the cheese.

Bake:
- Follow the pizza dough package instructions for baking. Typically, bake in a preheated oven until the crust is golden, and the cheese is melted and bubbly.

Garnish:
- Sprinkle sesame seeds over the baked pizza for added texture.
- Optionally, drizzle teriyaki sauce over the top for extra flavor.

Serve:
- Slice the Yakitori Quail Egg Pizza into portions and serve hot.

Enjoy the delicious combination of grilled yakitori chicken and quail eggs on your pizza! This fusion dish offers a unique twist on traditional flavors. Customize with additional toppings or add your favorite sauce for an extra layer of taste.

Soba Salad Pizza

Ingredients:

For the Soba Salad Topping:

- 1 cup cooked soba noodles, cooled
- 1/2 cup julienned carrots
- 1/2 cup sliced cucumber
- 1/4 cup sliced radishes
- 1/4 cup edamame, cooked and shelled
- 2 tablespoons sesame seeds
- 2 tablespoons chopped fresh cilantro or parsley

For the Pizza:

- 1 pizza dough (store-bought or homemade)
- 1/2 cup sesame ginger dressing
- 1 cup shredded cooked chicken (optional)

- 1 cup shredded mozzarella cheese
- 1/4 cup sliced green onions
- 1 tablespoon soy sauce (for drizzling)
- 1 tablespoon sesame oil (for drizzling)

Instructions:

For the Soba Salad Topping:

Prepare Soba Salad Topping:
- In a bowl, combine cooked soba noodles, julienned carrots, sliced cucumber, sliced radishes, edamame, sesame seeds, and chopped cilantro or parsley. Toss the ingredients until well combined.

For the Pizza:

Preheat Oven:
- Preheat your oven according to the pizza dough package instructions.

Roll Out Pizza Dough:
- Roll out the pizza dough on a floured surface to your desired thickness.

Assemble Pizza:
- Place the rolled-out dough on a pizza stone or baking sheet.
- Spread a layer of sesame ginger dressing evenly over the dough, leaving a small border around the edges.
- If using shredded chicken, distribute it evenly over the dressing.
- Sprinkle shredded mozzarella cheese over the pizza.
- Spoon the prepared soba salad topping over the cheese.
- Add sliced green onions on top.

Bake:
- Follow the pizza dough package instructions for baking. Typically, bake in a preheated oven until the crust is golden, and the cheese is melted and bubbly.

Drizzle:
- Drizzle soy sauce and sesame oil over the baked pizza for added flavor.

Serve:
- Slice the Soba Salad Pizza into portions and serve warm.

Enjoy the delightful combination of a refreshing soba noodle salad on a pizza! This fusion dish offers a unique blend of textures and flavors. Customize with additional toppings or adjust the drizzle to your liking.

Japanese Pumpkin (Kabocha) Pizza

Ingredients:

For the Kabocha Topping:

- 1 cup kabocha squash, peeled and thinly sliced
- 1 tablespoon olive oil
- Salt and pepper to taste
- 1 teaspoon soy sauce
- 1 teaspoon honey or maple syrup

For the Pizza:

- 1 pizza dough (store-bought or homemade)
- 1 cup shredded mozzarella cheese
- 1/4 cup crumbled feta cheese
- 1/4 cup caramelized onions
- 2 tablespoons toasted pine nuts
- Fresh thyme leaves for garnish
- Balsamic glaze for drizzling (optional)

Instructions:

For the Kabocha Topping:

Prepare Kabocha Squash:
- Preheat the oven to 400°F (200°C).
- Toss the thinly sliced kabocha squash with olive oil, salt, pepper, soy sauce, and honey or maple syrup until well coated.
- Spread the seasoned kabocha slices on a baking sheet in a single layer.
- Roast in the preheated oven for about 15-20 minutes or until the squash is tender and slightly caramelized. Set aside.

For the Pizza:

Preheat Oven:
- Preheat your oven according to the pizza dough package instructions.

Roll Out Pizza Dough:
- Roll out the pizza dough on a floured surface to your desired thickness.

Assemble Pizza:
- Place the rolled-out dough on a pizza stone or baking sheet.
- Sprinkle a layer of shredded mozzarella cheese over the dough.
- Distribute the roasted kabocha squash slices evenly over the cheese.
- Add crumbled feta cheese, caramelized onions, and toasted pine nuts as additional toppings.

Bake:
- Follow the pizza dough package instructions for baking. Typically, bake in a preheated oven until the crust is golden, and the cheese is melted and bubbly.

Garnish:
- Sprinkle fresh thyme leaves over the baked pizza for added freshness.
- Optionally, drizzle balsamic glaze over the top for a touch of sweetness and acidity.

Serve:
- Slice the Japanese Pumpkin Pizza into portions and serve warm.

Enjoy the unique and comforting flavor of kabocha squash on your pizza! This fusion dish offers a delightful combination of sweetness, creaminess, and earthiness. Customize with additional toppings or experiment with different cheeses for a personalized touch.

Teriyaki Tofu and Broccoli Pizza

Ingredients:

For the Teriyaki Tofu and Broccoli:

- 1 block firm tofu, pressed and cubed
- 1 cup broccoli florets
- 2 tablespoons teriyaki sauce
- 1 tablespoon soy sauce
- 1 tablespoon mirin
- 1 tablespoon vegetable oil

- 1 teaspoon sesame oil
- 1 teaspoon grated ginger
- 2 cloves garlic, minced

For the Pizza:

- 1 pizza dough (store-bought or homemade)
- 1 cup shredded mozzarella cheese
- 1/4 cup sliced red bell pepper
- 1/4 cup sliced green onions
- Sesame seeds for garnish
- Drizzle of extra teriyaki sauce for finishing

Instructions:

For the Teriyaki Tofu and Broccoli:

Prepare Teriyaki Tofu and Broccoli:
- In a bowl, mix together teriyaki sauce, soy sauce, mirin, vegetable oil, sesame oil, grated ginger, and minced garlic.
- Place the cubed tofu in the marinade and let it soak for at least 15-20 minutes.
- In a skillet over medium heat, stir-fry marinated tofu until it's golden and slightly crispy.
- Add broccoli florets to the skillet and continue stir-frying until the broccoli is tender-crisp.

For the Pizza:

Preheat Oven:
- Preheat your oven according to the pizza dough package instructions.

Roll Out Pizza Dough:
- Roll out the pizza dough on a floured surface to your desired thickness.

Assemble Pizza:
- Place the rolled-out dough on a pizza stone or baking sheet.
- Sprinkle a layer of shredded mozzarella cheese over the dough.
- Distribute the teriyaki tofu and broccoli mixture evenly over the cheese.
- Add sliced red bell pepper and sliced green onions as additional toppings.

Bake:

- Follow the pizza dough package instructions for baking. Typically, bake in a preheated oven until the crust is golden, and the cheese is melted and bubbly.

Garnish:
- Sprinkle sesame seeds over the baked pizza for added texture.
- Drizzle extra teriyaki sauce over the top for an extra burst of flavor.

Serve:
- Slice the Teriyaki Tofu and Broccoli Pizza into portions and serve hot.

Enjoy the delightful combination of teriyaki-infused tofu, broccoli, and vegetables on your pizza! This fusion dish offers a perfect balance of sweet, savory, and umami flavors. Customize with additional toppings or drizzle extra teriyaki sauce for an extra kick.

Sesame-Crusted Salmon Pizza

Ingredients:

For the Sesame-Crusted Salmon:

- 2 salmon fillets, skin removed
- 2 tablespoons soy sauce
- 1 tablespoon sesame oil
- 1 tablespoon honey or maple syrup
- 1 tablespoon rice vinegar
- 1 tablespoon black and white sesame seeds
- 1 teaspoon grated ginger
- 1 teaspoon minced garlic

For the Pizza:

- 1 pizza dough (store-bought or homemade)
- 1/2 cup cream cheese or whipped cream cheese
- 1 cup shredded mozzarella cheese
- 1/4 cup thinly sliced red onion
- 1/4 cup sliced cucumber
- 1/4 cup sliced avocado
- Fresh cilantro or parsley for garnish
- Extra sesame seeds for garnish
- Soy sauce for drizzling

Instructions:

For the Sesame-Crusted Salmon:

Prepare Sesame-Crusted Salmon:
- In a bowl, whisk together soy sauce, sesame oil, honey or maple syrup, rice vinegar, sesame seeds, grated ginger, and minced garlic.
- Place the salmon fillets in a shallow dish and pour the marinade over them, ensuring they are well-coated.
- Marinate the salmon in the refrigerator for at least 30 minutes.
- Preheat the oven to 400°F (200°C).
- Remove the salmon from the marinade and coat each fillet with additional sesame seeds.
- Bake in the preheated oven for about 12-15 minutes or until the salmon is cooked through and flakes easily.

For the Pizza:

Preheat Oven:
- Preheat your oven according to the pizza dough package instructions.

Roll Out Pizza Dough:
- Roll out the pizza dough on a floured surface to your desired thickness.

Assemble Pizza:
- Place the rolled-out dough on a pizza stone or baking sheet.
- Spread a layer of cream cheese over the dough.
- Sprinkle shredded mozzarella cheese over the cream cheese.
- Flake the cooked sesame-crusted salmon over the cheese.
- Add thinly sliced red onion, sliced cucumber, and sliced avocado as additional toppings.

Bake:
- Follow the pizza dough package instructions for baking. Typically, bake in a preheated oven until the crust is golden, and the cheese is melted and bubbly.

Garnish:
- Garnish the Sesame-Crusted Salmon Pizza with fresh cilantro or parsley and extra sesame seeds.

Drizzle:
- Drizzle soy sauce over the top for an extra burst of umami flavor.

Serve:
- Slice the pizza into portions and serve hot.

Enjoy the delicious combination of sesame-crusted salmon and fresh vegetables on your pizza! This fusion dish offers a perfect blend of textures and flavors. Customize with additional toppings or drizzle extra soy sauce for an extra kick.

Yuzu-Honey Chicken Pizza

Ingredients:

For the Yuzu-Honey Chicken:

- 1 cup cooked and shredded chicken (rotisserie or grilled)
- 2 tablespoons yuzu juice (substitute with a mix of lemon and lime juice if yuzu is unavailable)
- 1 tablespoon honey
- 1 tablespoon soy sauce
- 1 tablespoon sesame oil
- 1 teaspoon grated ginger
- 1 teaspoon minced garlic
- 1 tablespoon chopped green onions

For the Pizza:

- 1 pizza dough (store-bought or homemade)
- 1 cup shredded mozzarella cheese
- 1/4 cup sliced red bell pepper
- 1/4 cup sliced yellow bell pepper
- 1/4 cup sliced red onion
- 1 tablespoon sesame seeds
- Fresh cilantro for garnish

Instructions:

For the Yuzu-Honey Chicken:

   Prepare Yuzu-Honey Chicken:
   - In a bowl, whisk together yuzu juice, honey, soy sauce, sesame oil, grated ginger, minced garlic, and chopped green onions.
   - Add the shredded chicken to the marinade, ensuring it is well-coated.
   - Let the chicken marinate for at least 15-20 minutes.

For the Pizza:

   Preheat Oven:
   - Preheat your oven according to the pizza dough package instructions.

   Roll Out Pizza Dough:

- Roll out the pizza dough on a floured surface to your desired thickness.

Assemble Pizza:
- Place the rolled-out dough on a pizza stone or baking sheet.
- Sprinkle a layer of shredded mozzarella cheese over the dough.
- Distribute the marinated yuzu-honey chicken evenly over the cheese.
- Add sliced red and yellow bell peppers and sliced red onion as additional toppings.

Bake:
- Follow the pizza dough package instructions for baking. Typically, bake in a preheated oven until the crust is golden, and the cheese is melted and bubbly.

Garnish:
- Sprinkle sesame seeds over the baked pizza for added texture.
- Garnish with fresh cilantro.

Serve:
- Slice the Yuzu-Honey Chicken Pizza into portions and serve hot.

Enjoy the vibrant and citrusy flavors of yuzu combined with the sweetness of honey on your pizza! This fusion dish offers a unique and refreshing twist. Customize with additional toppings or drizzle extra yuzu-honey sauce for an extra burst of flavor.

Japanese Pickles Pizza

Ingredients:

For the Japanese Pickles:

- 1 cup assorted Japanese pickles (daikon radish, cucumbers, carrots, etc.), thinly sliced
- 1 tablespoon rice vinegar
- 1 tablespoon soy sauce
- 1 teaspoon sugar
- 1/2 teaspoon sesame oil

For the Pizza:

- 1 pizza dough (store-bought or homemade)
- 1 cup shredded mozzarella cheese
- 1/4 cup cream cheese or whipped cream cheese
- 1/4 cup sliced red onion
- 1/4 cup sliced shiitake mushrooms
- 1 tablespoon sesame seeds
- Fresh cilantro or shiso leaves for garnish

Instructions:

For the Japanese Pickles:

Prepare Japanese Pickles:
- In a bowl, combine thinly sliced Japanese pickles with rice vinegar, soy sauce, sugar, and sesame oil.
- Toss the pickles until they are well-coated with the marinade.
- Let the pickles marinate for at least 15-20 minutes.

For the Pizza:

Preheat Oven:
- Preheat your oven according to the pizza dough package instructions.

Roll Out Pizza Dough:
- Roll out the pizza dough on a floured surface to your desired thickness.

Assemble Pizza:
- Place the rolled-out dough on a pizza stone or baking sheet.

- Spread a layer of cream cheese over the dough.
- Sprinkle shredded mozzarella cheese over the cream cheese.
- Distribute the marinated Japanese pickles evenly over the cheese.
- Add sliced red onion and sliced shiitake mushrooms as additional toppings.

Bake:
- Follow the pizza dough package instructions for baking. Typically, bake in a preheated oven until the crust is golden, and the cheese is melted and bubbly.

Garnish:
- Sprinkle sesame seeds over the baked pizza for added texture.
- Garnish with fresh cilantro or shiso leaves.

Serve:
- Slice the Japanese Pickles Pizza into portions and serve hot.

Enjoy the unique and tangy flavor of Japanese pickles on your pizza! This fusion dish offers a delightful contrast of textures and tastes. Customize with additional toppings or experiment with different pickles for a personalized touch.

Tonkatsu Pork Pizza

Ingredients:

For the Tonkatsu Pork:

- 2 pork loin or pork tenderloin slices
- Salt and pepper to taste
- Flour for dredging
- 1-2 eggs, beaten
- Panko breadcrumbs
- Vegetable oil for frying

For the Pizza:

- 1 pizza dough (store-bought or homemade)
- Tonkatsu sauce (store-bought or homemade)
- 1 cup shredded mozzarella cheese
- 1/4 cup shredded cabbage
- 1/4 cup thinly sliced red onion
- 2 tablespoons sliced green onions
- Toasted sesame seeds for garnish
- Japanese mayonnaise for drizzling (optional)

Instructions:

For the Tonkatsu Pork:

Prepare Tonkatsu Pork:
- Season pork slices with salt and pepper.
- Dredge each pork slice in flour, dip into beaten eggs, and coat with Panko breadcrumbs, pressing the breadcrumbs onto the pork to adhere.
- Heat vegetable oil in a skillet over medium heat.
- Fry the breaded pork slices until golden brown and cooked through. Transfer to a paper towel-lined plate to drain excess oil.
- Once cooled, slice the tonkatsu into thin strips.

For the Pizza:

- Preheat Oven:
  - Preheat your oven according to the pizza dough package instructions.
- Roll Out Pizza Dough:
  - Roll out the pizza dough on a floured surface to your desired thickness.
- Assemble Pizza:
  - Place the rolled-out dough on a pizza stone or baking sheet.
  - Spread a layer of tonkatsu sauce over the dough.
  - Sprinkle shredded mozzarella cheese over the tonkatsu sauce.
  - Distribute the sliced tonkatsu pork, shredded cabbage, and sliced red onion evenly over the cheese.
- Bake:
  - Follow the pizza dough package instructions for baking. Typically, bake in a preheated oven until the crust is golden, and the cheese is melted and bubbly.
- Garnish:
  - Sprinkle sliced green onions and toasted sesame seeds over the baked pizza.
  - Optionally, drizzle Japanese mayonnaise over the top for an extra layer of creaminess.
- Serve:
  - Slice the Tonkatsu Pork Pizza into portions and serve hot.

Enjoy the crunchy and savory goodness of tonkatsu on your pizza! This fusion dish offers a delightful blend of textures and flavors. Customize with additional toppings or adjust the drizzle to your liking.

Soy-Ginger Scallops Pizza

Ingredients:

For the Soy-Ginger Scallops:

- 1/2 pound fresh scallops, patted dry
- 2 tablespoons soy sauce
- 1 tablespoon rice vinegar
- 1 tablespoon honey or maple syrup
- 1 tablespoon sesame oil
- 1 tablespoon grated ginger
- 2 cloves garlic, minced
- 1 tablespoon chopped green onions
- Sesame seeds for garnish

For the Pizza:

- 1 pizza dough (store-bought or homemade)
- 1 cup shredded mozzarella cheese
- 1/4 cup sliced red bell pepper
- 1/4 cup sliced yellow bell pepper
- 1/4 cup sliced green onions
- 1 tablespoon sesame seeds for garnish
- Fresh cilantro for garnish
- Sriracha or chili oil for drizzling (optional)

Instructions:

For the Soy-Ginger Scallops:

    Prepare Soy-Ginger Scallops:

- In a bowl, whisk together soy sauce, rice vinegar, honey or maple syrup, sesame oil, grated ginger, minced garlic, and chopped green onions.
- Add the scallops to the marinade, ensuring they are well-coated. Let them marinate for about 15-20 minutes.
- Heat a skillet over medium-high heat and sear the scallops for 1-2 minutes on each side until they develop a golden crust. Set aside.

For the Pizza:

Preheat Oven:
- Preheat your oven according to the pizza dough package instructions.

Roll Out Pizza Dough:
- Roll out the pizza dough on a floured surface to your desired thickness.

Assemble Pizza:
- Place the rolled-out dough on a pizza stone or baking sheet.
- Sprinkle a layer of shredded mozzarella cheese over the dough.
- Distribute the seared soy-ginger scallops evenly over the cheese.
- Add sliced red and yellow bell peppers and sliced green onions as additional toppings.

Bake:
- Follow the pizza dough package instructions for baking. Typically, bake in a preheated oven until the crust is golden, and the cheese is melted and bubbly.

Garnish:
- Sprinkle sesame seeds over the baked pizza for added texture.
- Garnish with fresh cilantro.

Drizzle:
- Optionally, drizzle Sriracha or chili oil over the top for a spicy kick.

Serve:
- Slice the Soy-Ginger Scallops Pizza into portions and serve hot.

Enjoy the delicious combination of soy-ginger scallops and fresh vegetables on your pizza! This fusion dish offers a perfect balance of savory, sweet, and spicy flavors. Customize with additional toppings or adjust the drizzle to your liking.

Natto and Shiso Pizza

Ingredients:

For the Natto and Shiso Topping:

- 1 cup natto (fermented soybeans), prepared according to package instructions
- 1 tablespoon soy sauce
- 1 tablespoon mirin
- 1 teaspoon sesame oil
- 1 teaspoon grated ginger
- 2 cloves garlic, minced
- 1 tablespoon chopped green onions
- Shiso leaves, chopped or whole, for topping

For the Pizza:

- 1 pizza dough (store-bought or homemade)
- 1 cup shredded mozzarella cheese
- 1/4 cup crumbled feta cheese (optional for extra creaminess)
- 1/4 cup sliced red onion
- 1/4 cup sliced bell peppers (any color)
- 1 tablespoon sesame seeds
- Soy sauce for drizzling

Instructions:

For the Natto and Shiso Topping:

Prepare Natto and Shiso Topping:
- In a bowl, combine natto with soy sauce, mirin, sesame oil, grated ginger, minced garlic, and chopped green onions. Mix well.

For the Pizza:

Preheat Oven:
- Preheat your oven according to the pizza dough package instructions.

Roll Out Pizza Dough:
- Roll out the pizza dough on a floured surface to your desired thickness.

Assemble Pizza:
- Place the rolled-out dough on a pizza stone or baking sheet.
- Spread a layer of shredded mozzarella cheese over the dough.
- Optionally, sprinkle crumbled feta cheese for extra creaminess.
- Distribute the prepared natto and shiso mixture evenly over the cheese.
- Add sliced red onion and bell peppers as additional toppings.

Bake:
- Follow the pizza dough package instructions for baking. Typically, bake in a preheated oven until the crust is golden, and the cheese is melted and bubbly.

Garnish:
- Sprinkle sesame seeds over the baked pizza for added texture.
- Place chopped or whole shiso leaves on top for a fresh and aromatic touch.

Drizzle:
- Drizzle soy sauce over the top for an extra burst of umami flavor.

Serve:
- Slice the Natto and Shiso Pizza into portions and serve hot.

Enjoy the unique combination of natto and shiso on your pizza! This fusion dish offers a bold and distinctive flavor profile. Customize with additional toppings or adjust the drizzle to your liking.

Sesame Asparagus and Egg Pizza

Ingredients:

For the Sesame Asparagus and Egg Topping:

- 1 bunch asparagus, tough ends trimmed
- 1 tablespoon sesame oil
- Salt and pepper to taste
- 2 tablespoons sesame seeds
- 4 large eggs

For the Pizza:

- 1 pizza dough (store-bought or homemade)
- 1 cup shredded mozzarella cheese
- 1/4 cup grated Parmesan cheese
- 1 tablespoon olive oil
- Red pepper flakes for a touch of heat (optional)
- Fresh chives or green onions, chopped, for garnish

Instructions:

For the Sesame Asparagus and Egg Topping:

   Prepare Sesame Asparagus and Egg Topping:
   - Preheat the oven to 400°F (200°C).
   - Toss asparagus spears in sesame oil, salt, and pepper.

- Roast the asparagus in the preheated oven for about 10-12 minutes or until tender-crisp.
- Sprinkle sesame seeds over the roasted asparagus during the last 5 minutes of roasting.
- Meanwhile, fry or poach eggs to your desired doneness.

For the Pizza:

Preheat Oven:
- Preheat your oven according to the pizza dough package instructions.

Roll Out Pizza Dough:
- Roll out the pizza dough on a floured surface to your desired thickness.

Assemble Pizza:
- Place the rolled-out dough on a pizza stone or baking sheet.
- Sprinkle a layer of shredded mozzarella cheese over the dough.
- Add the roasted sesame asparagus evenly over the cheese.
- Carefully place the fried or poached eggs on top.
- Sprinkle grated Parmesan cheese over the pizza.
- Drizzle olive oil over the toppings.
- Optionally, add red pepper flakes for a touch of heat.

Bake:
- Follow the pizza dough package instructions for baking. Typically, bake in a preheated oven until the crust is golden, and the cheese is melted and bubbly.

Garnish:
- Sprinkle chopped fresh chives or green onions over the baked pizza.

Serve:
- Slice the Sesame Asparagus and Egg Pizza into portions and serve hot.

Enjoy the combination of sesame-infused asparagus and runny eggs on your pizza! This fusion dish offers a delightful mix of textures and flavors. Customize with additional toppings or adjust the spice level to your liking.

Miso Maple Bacon Pizza

Ingredients:

For the Miso Maple Bacon Sauce:

- 2 tablespoons white miso paste
- 2 tablespoons maple syrup
- 1 tablespoon soy sauce
- 1 tablespoon rice vinegar
- 1 teaspoon sesame oil
- 1 teaspoon minced garlic
- 1/2 teaspoon grated ginger

For the Pizza:

- 1 pizza dough (store-bought or homemade)
- 1 cup shredded mozzarella cheese
- 1/2 cup cooked and crumbled bacon
- 1/4 cup sliced red onion
- 2 tablespoons chopped scallions (green parts)
- 1 tablespoon sesame seeds
- Fresh cilantro for garnish (optional)

Instructions:

For the Miso Maple Bacon Sauce:

Prepare Miso Maple Bacon Sauce:
- In a bowl, whisk together white miso paste, maple syrup, soy sauce, rice vinegar, sesame oil, minced garlic, and grated ginger. Adjust the sweetness and saltiness to your liking.

For the Pizza:

Preheat Oven:
- Preheat your oven according to the pizza dough package instructions.

Roll Out Pizza Dough:
- Roll out the pizza dough on a floured surface to your desired thickness.

Assemble Pizza:
- Place the rolled-out dough on a pizza stone or baking sheet.
- Spread a layer of the prepared miso maple bacon sauce over the dough.
- Sprinkle a layer of shredded mozzarella cheese over the sauce.
- Distribute the cooked and crumbled bacon evenly over the cheese.
- Add sliced red onion and chopped scallions as additional toppings.

Bake:
- Follow the pizza dough package instructions for baking. Typically, bake in a preheated oven until the crust is golden, and the cheese is melted and bubbly.

Garnish:
- Sprinkle sesame seeds over the baked pizza for added texture.
- Optionally, garnish with fresh cilantro for a burst of freshness.

Serve:
- Slice the Miso Maple Bacon Pizza into portions and serve hot.

Enjoy the rich and savory combination of miso maple bacon on your pizza! This fusion dish offers a unique blend of flavors. Customize with additional toppings or experiment with different cheeses for a personalized touch.

Ginger Miso Chicken Pizza

Ingredients:

For the Ginger Miso Chicken:

- 1 cup cooked and shredded chicken
- 2 tablespoons white miso paste
- 1 tablespoon soy sauce
- 1 tablespoon rice vinegar
- 1 tablespoon honey or maple syrup
- 1 tablespoon sesame oil
- 1 tablespoon grated ginger
- 1 teaspoon minced garlic
- 2 tablespoons chopped green onions

For the Pizza:

- 1 pizza dough (store-bought or homemade)
- 1 cup shredded mozzarella cheese
- 1/4 cup sliced red bell pepper
- 1/4 cup sliced yellow bell pepper
- 1/4 cup sliced shiitake mushrooms

- 1 tablespoon sesame seeds
- Fresh cilantro for garnish

Instructions:

For the Ginger Miso Chicken:

Prepare Ginger Miso Chicken:
- In a bowl, whisk together white miso paste, soy sauce, rice vinegar, honey or maple syrup, sesame oil, grated ginger, minced garlic, and chopped green onions.
- Add the shredded chicken to the miso mixture and toss until well-coated.

For the Pizza:

Preheat Oven:
- Preheat your oven according to the pizza dough package instructions.

Roll Out Pizza Dough:
- Roll out the pizza dough on a floured surface to your desired thickness.

Assemble Pizza:
- Place the rolled-out dough on a pizza stone or baking sheet.
- Spread a layer of shredded mozzarella cheese over the dough.
- Distribute the ginger miso chicken mixture evenly over the cheese.
- Add sliced red and yellow bell peppers and sliced shiitake mushrooms as additional toppings.

Bake:
- Follow the pizza dough package instructions for baking. Typically, bake in a preheated oven until the crust is golden, and the cheese is melted and bubbly.

Garnish:
- Sprinkle sesame seeds over the baked pizza for added texture.
- Garnish with fresh cilantro for a burst of freshness.

Serve:
- Slice the Ginger Miso Chicken Pizza into portions and serve hot.

Enjoy the delightful combination of ginger miso chicken and colorful vegetables on your pizza! This fusion dish offers a harmonious blend of flavors. Customize with additional toppings or adjust the ginger and miso to your liking.

Yuzu Pepper Tuna Tataki Pizza

Ingredients:

For the Yuzu Pepper Tuna Tataki:

- 1/2 pound sushi-grade tuna
- 2 tablespoons yuzu juice
- 1 tablespoon soy sauce
- 1 teaspoon yuzu pepper paste (adjust to taste)
- 1 tablespoon sesame oil
- 1 teaspoon grated ginger
- 1 teaspoon honey
- 1 tablespoon chopped green onions
- 1 tablespoon sesame seeds
- Salt and pepper to taste

For the Pizza:

- 1 pizza dough (store-bought or homemade)
- 1 cup shredded mozzarella cheese
- 1/4 cup sliced red onion
- 1/4 cup sliced cucumber
- 1 tablespoon chopped cilantro
- Yuzu mayonnaise for drizzling (optional)

Instructions:

For the Yuzu Pepper Tuna Tataki:

Prepare Yuzu Pepper Tuna Tataki:
- Pat dry the tuna with paper towels and season with salt and pepper.
- In a bowl, mix yuzu juice, soy sauce, yuzu pepper paste, sesame oil, grated ginger, honey, chopped green onions, and sesame seeds to create the marinade.
- Heat a skillet over high heat. Sear the tuna for about 30 seconds to 1 minute on each side. The goal is to sear the edges while keeping the inside raw.
- Slice the seared tuna thinly.

For the Pizza:

Preheat Oven:
- Preheat your oven according to the pizza dough package instructions.

Roll Out Pizza Dough:
- Roll out the pizza dough on a floured surface to your desired thickness.

Assemble Pizza:
- Place the rolled-out dough on a pizza stone or baking sheet.
- Sprinkle a layer of shredded mozzarella cheese over the dough.
- Distribute the sliced tuna tataki evenly over the cheese.
- Add sliced red onion and sliced cucumber as additional toppings.

Bake:
- Follow the pizza dough package instructions for baking. Typically, bake in a preheated oven until the crust is golden, and the cheese is melted and bubbly.

Garnish:
- Sprinkle chopped cilantro over the baked pizza.
- Optionally, drizzle yuzu mayonnaise over the top for extra creaminess and flavor.

Serve:
- Slice the Yuzu Pepper Tuna Tataki Pizza into portions and serve hot.

Enjoy the vibrant and citrusy flavors of yuzu pepper tuna tataki on your pizza! This fusion dish offers a perfect balance of freshness and umami. Customize with additional toppings or adjust the drizzle to your liking.

Wasabi Edamame Hummus Pizza

Ingredients:

For the Wasabi Edamame Hummus:
- 1 cup shelled edamame, cooked
- 2 tablespoons tahini
- 1 tablespoon soy sauce
- 1 tablespoon rice vinegar
- 1 tablespoon sesame oil
- 1 teaspoon wasabi paste (adjust to taste)

- 1 clove garlic, minced
- 2 tablespoons water (adjust for desired consistency)
- Salt and pepper to taste

For the Pizza:

- 1 pizza dough (store-bought or homemade)
- 1 cup shredded mozzarella cheese
- 1/4 cup sliced red bell pepper
- 1/4 cup sliced yellow bell pepper
- 1/4 cup sliced cucumber
- 1/4 cup sliced radishes
- 2 tablespoons chopped green onions
- Sesame seeds for garnish

Instructions:

For the Wasabi Edamame Hummus:

Prepare Wasabi Edamame Hummus:
- In a food processor, combine cooked edamame, tahini, soy sauce, rice vinegar, sesame oil, wasabi paste, minced garlic, water, salt, and pepper.
- Blend until smooth, adding more water if necessary to reach your desired hummus consistency. Adjust the taste by adding more wasabi, soy sauce, or salt as needed.

For the Pizza:

Preheat Oven:
- Preheat your oven according to the pizza dough package instructions.

Roll Out Pizza Dough:
- Roll out the pizza dough on a floured surface to your desired thickness.

Assemble Pizza:
- Place the rolled-out dough on a pizza stone or baking sheet.
- Spread a layer of the prepared wasabi edamame hummus over the dough.
- Sprinkle a layer of shredded mozzarella cheese over the hummus.
- Add sliced red and yellow bell peppers, sliced cucumber, and sliced radishes as toppings.

Bake:

- Follow the pizza dough package instructions for baking. Typically, bake in a preheated oven until the crust is golden, and the cheese is melted and bubbly.

Garnish:
- Sprinkle chopped green onions and sesame seeds over the baked pizza.

Serve:
- Slice the Wasabi Edamame Hummus Pizza into portions and serve hot.

Enjoy the unique and flavorful combination of wasabi-infused edamame hummus and fresh vegetables on your pizza! This fusion dish offers a perfect balance of creaminess and kick. Customize with additional toppings or adjust the hummus spice level to your liking.

Sukiyaki Beef and Onion Pizza

Ingredients:

For the Sukiyaki Beef:

- 1/2 pound thinly sliced beef (such as ribeye or sirloin)
- 1/4 cup soy sauce
- 2 tablespoons mirin

- 2 tablespoons sake
- 1 tablespoon sugar
- 1 tablespoon sesame oil
- 1 onion, thinly sliced
- 1 cup shiitake mushrooms, sliced
- 1 cup napa cabbage, chopped

For the Pizza:

- 1 pizza dough (store-bought or homemade)
- 1 cup shredded mozzarella cheese
- 1/4 cup sliced green onions
- 1 tablespoon sesame seeds
- Shichimi togarashi (Japanese seven spice) for added heat (optional)

Instructions:

For the Sukiyaki Beef:

Prepare Sukiyaki Beef:
- In a bowl, mix soy sauce, mirin, sake, and sugar to create the sukiyaki sauce.
- Heat sesame oil in a skillet over medium-high heat.
- Add thinly sliced beef to the skillet and cook until browned.
- Add sliced onions, shiitake mushrooms, and napa cabbage to the skillet.
- Pour the sukiyaki sauce over the ingredients and stir-fry until vegetables are tender and the sauce has caramelized slightly.

For the Pizza:

Preheat Oven:
- Preheat your oven according to the pizza dough package instructions.

Roll Out Pizza Dough:
- Roll out the pizza dough on a floured surface to your desired thickness.

Assemble Pizza:
- Place the rolled-out dough on a pizza stone or baking sheet.
- Sprinkle a layer of shredded mozzarella cheese over the dough.
- Distribute the cooked sukiyaki beef and vegetable mixture evenly over the cheese.
- Sprinkle sliced green onions and sesame seeds over the toppings.
- Optionally, sprinkle shichimi togarashi for added heat.

Bake:
- Follow the pizza dough package instructions for baking. Typically, bake in a preheated oven until the crust is golden, and the cheese is melted and bubbly.

Serve:
- Slice the Sukiyaki Beef and Onion Pizza into portions and serve hot.

Enjoy the savory and umami-packed flavors of sukiyaki beef on your pizza! This fusion dish offers a unique twist on traditional pizza toppings. Customize with additional toppings or adjust the spice level to your liking.

Yakitori Pineapple Teriyaki Pizza

Ingredients:

For the Yakitori Chicken:

- 1 pound boneless, skinless chicken thighs, cut into bite-sized pieces
- 1/4 cup soy sauce
- 2 tablespoons sake
- 2 tablespoons mirin
- 1 tablespoon sugar
- Bamboo skewers, soaked in water

For the Pizza:

- 1 pizza dough (store-bought or homemade)
- 1 cup shredded mozzarella cheese
- 1/2 cup teriyaki sauce (store-bought or homemade)
- 1 cup pineapple chunks
- 1/4 cup sliced red bell pepper
- 2 tablespoons chopped green onions
- Sesame seeds for garnish

Instructions:

For the Yakitori Chicken:

Prepare Yakitori Chicken:
- In a bowl, mix soy sauce, sake, mirin, and sugar to create the yakitori marinade.
- Thread chicken pieces onto soaked bamboo skewers.
- Brush the chicken skewers with the yakitori marinade.
- Grill or broil the skewers until the chicken is cooked and has a nice char. Baste with the marinade during grilling.

For the Pizza:

Preheat Oven:
- Preheat your oven according to the pizza dough package instructions.

Roll Out Pizza Dough:
- Roll out the pizza dough on a floured surface to your desired thickness.

Assemble Pizza:
- Place the rolled-out dough on a pizza stone or baking sheet.
- Spread a layer of teriyaki sauce over the dough.
- Sprinkle a layer of shredded mozzarella cheese over the teriyaki sauce.
- Distribute the grilled yakitori chicken evenly over the cheese.
- Add pineapple chunks and sliced red bell pepper as additional toppings.

Bake:
- Follow the pizza dough package instructions for baking. Typically, bake in a preheated oven until the crust is golden, and the cheese is melted and bubbly.

Garnish:
- Sprinkle chopped green onions and sesame seeds over the baked pizza.

Serve:
- Slice the Yakitori Pineapple Teriyaki Pizza into portions and serve hot.

Enjoy the delightful combination of yakitori chicken, sweet pineapple, and teriyaki sauce on your pizza! This fusion dish offers a perfect blend of flavors. Customize with additional toppings or drizzle extra teriyaki sauce for an added burst of taste.

Udon Noodle Pizza

Ingredients:

For the Udon Noodles:

- 8 ounces udon noodles, cooked according to package instructions
- 2 tablespoons soy sauce
- 1 tablespoon sesame oil
- 1 tablespoon mirin
- 1 tablespoon rice vinegar
- 1 teaspoon sugar
- 1 clove garlic, minced
- 1 teaspoon grated ginger

For the Pizza:

- 1 pizza dough (store-bought or homemade)
- 1/2 cup hoisin sauce
- 1 cup shredded mozzarella cheese
- 1/2 cup shredded cooked chicken or tofu
- 1/4 cup sliced red bell pepper
- 1/4 cup sliced shiitake mushrooms
- 2 tablespoons chopped green onions
- Sesame seeds for garnish

Instructions:

For the Udon Noodles:

Prepare Udon Noodles:
- Cook udon noodles according to package instructions. Drain and set aside.
- In a bowl, mix soy sauce, sesame oil, mirin, rice vinegar, sugar, minced garlic, and grated ginger.
- Toss the cooked udon noodles in the sauce mixture until well-coated. Set aside.

For the Pizza:

Preheat Oven:
- Preheat your oven according to the pizza dough package instructions.

Roll Out Pizza Dough:

- Roll out the pizza dough on a floured surface to your desired thickness.

Assemble Pizza:
- Place the rolled-out dough on a pizza stone or baking sheet.
- Spread hoisin sauce evenly over the dough.
- Sprinkle a layer of shredded mozzarella cheese over the hoisin sauce.
- Distribute the sauced udon noodles, shredded cooked chicken or tofu, sliced red bell pepper, and sliced shiitake mushrooms evenly over the cheese.

Bake:
- Follow the pizza dough package instructions for baking. Typically, bake in a preheated oven until the crust is golden, and the cheese is melted and bubbly.

Garnish:
- Sprinkle chopped green onions and sesame seeds over the baked pizza.

Serve:
- Slice the Udon Noodle Pizza into portions and serve hot.

Enjoy the unique combination of udon noodles and pizza flavors! This fusion dish offers a delightful mix of textures and tastes. Customize with additional toppings or drizzle extra hoisin sauce for added flavor.

Match White Chocolate Dessert Pizza

Ingredients:

For the Matcha White Chocolate Sauce:

- 1/2 cup white chocolate chips
- 1 tablespoon unsalted butter
- 1 teaspoon matcha powder
- 1/4 cup condensed milk

For the Pizza:

- 1 pizza dough (store-bought or homemade)
- 1 cup white chocolate chips
- 2 tablespoons matcha powder (for dusting)
- Fresh strawberries, sliced
- Fresh mint leaves for garnish (optional)

Instructions:

For the Matcha White Chocolate Sauce:

Prepare Matcha White Chocolate Sauce:
- In a small saucepan over low heat, melt white chocolate chips and butter, stirring continuously.
- Once melted, add matcha powder and condensed milk. Continue stirring until smooth and well combined.
- Remove from heat and let it cool slightly.

For the Pizza:

Preheat Oven:
- Preheat your oven according to the pizza dough package instructions.

Roll Out Pizza Dough:
- Roll out the pizza dough on a floured surface to your desired thickness.

Assemble Pizza:

- Place the rolled-out dough on a pizza stone or baking sheet.
- Spread the prepared Matcha White Chocolate Sauce evenly over the dough, leaving a small border around the edges.
- Sprinkle white chocolate chips over the sauce.
- Bake according to the pizza dough package instructions until the crust is golden, and the chocolate is melted.

Garnish:
- Once out of the oven, dust the pizza with matcha powder for an extra pop of flavor.
- Arrange fresh strawberry slices on top.
- Optionally, garnish with fresh mint leaves for a burst of freshness.

Serve:
- Slice the Matcha White Chocolate Dessert Pizza into portions and serve warm.

Enjoy the delightful combination of matcha and white chocolate on your dessert pizza!

Customize with additional toppings like whipped cream or vanilla ice cream for an extra treat. This fusion dish offers a perfect balance of sweetness and earthy notes.

Tofu Katsu Pizza

Ingredients:

For the Tofu Katsu:

- 1 block firm tofu, pressed and sliced into thick rectangles
- Salt and pepper to taste
- 1/2 cup all-purpose flour
- 2 eggs, beaten
- 1 cup panko breadcrumbs
- Vegetable oil for frying

For the Pizza:

- 1 pizza dough (store-bought or homemade)
- 1/2 cup tonkatsu sauce (store-bought or homemade)
- 1 cup shredded mozzarella cheese
- 1/4 cup shredded cabbage
- 1/4 cup julienned carrots
- 2 tablespoons chopped green onions
- Toasted sesame seeds for garnish

Instructions:

For the Tofu Katsu:

Prepare Tofu Katsu:
- Season tofu slices with salt and pepper.
- Dredge each tofu slice in flour, dip into beaten eggs, and coat with panko breadcrumbs, pressing the breadcrumbs onto the tofu to adhere.
- Heat vegetable oil in a skillet over medium heat.
- Fry the breaded tofu slices until golden brown and crispy. Transfer to a paper towel-lined plate to drain excess oil.

For the Pizza:

- Preheat Oven:
    - Preheat your oven according to the pizza dough package instructions.
- Roll Out Pizza Dough:
    - Roll out the pizza dough on a floured surface to your desired thickness.
- Assemble Pizza:
    - Place the rolled-out dough on a pizza stone or baking sheet.
    - Spread tonkatsu sauce evenly over the dough.
    - Sprinkle a layer of shredded mozzarella cheese over the sauce.
    - Distribute the crispy tofu katsu slices evenly over the cheese.
    - Add shredded cabbage, julienned carrots, and chopped green onions as additional toppings.
- Bake:
    - Follow the pizza dough package instructions for baking. Typically, bake in a preheated oven until the crust is golden, and the cheese is melted and bubbly.
- Garnish:
    - Sprinkle toasted sesame seeds over the baked pizza for added texture.
- Serve:
    - Slice the Tofu Katsu Pizza into portions and serve hot.

Enjoy the unique fusion of Japanese flavors with the crispy tofu katsu on your pizza! Customize with additional toppings or drizzle extra tonkatsu sauce for an extra burst of flavor.

Yakitori Beef and Shishito Pepper Pizza

Ingredients:

For the Yakitori Beef:

- 1/2 pound thinly sliced beef (such as ribeye or sirloin)
- 1/4 cup soy sauce
- 2 tablespoons mirin
- 2 tablespoons sake
- 1 tablespoon sugar
- Bamboo skewers, soaked in water

For the Pizza:

- 1 pizza dough (store-bought or homemade)
- 1 cup shredded mozzarella cheese
- 1/2 cup yakitori sauce (store-bought or homemade)
- 1 cup shishito peppers, sliced
- 1/4 cup sliced red onion
- 2 tablespoons chopped green onions
- Sesame seeds for garnish

Instructions:

For the Yakitori Beef:

Prepare Yakitori Beef:
- In a bowl, mix soy sauce, mirin, sake, and sugar to create the yakitori marinade.
- Thread beef slices onto soaked bamboo skewers.
- Brush the beef skewers with the yakitori marinade.
- Grill or broil the skewers until the beef is cooked and has a nice char. Baste with the marinade during grilling.
- Remove beef from skewers and slice thinly.

For the Pizza:

- Preheat Oven:
  - Preheat your oven according to the pizza dough package instructions.
- Roll Out Pizza Dough:
  - Roll out the pizza dough on a floured surface to your desired thickness.
- Assemble Pizza:
  - Place the rolled-out dough on a pizza stone or baking sheet.
  - Spread yakitori sauce evenly over the dough.
  - Sprinkle a layer of shredded mozzarella cheese over the sauce.
  - Distribute the sliced yakitori beef, sliced shishito peppers, and sliced red onion evenly over the cheese.
- Bake:
  - Follow the pizza dough package instructions for baking. Typically, bake in a preheated oven until the crust is golden, and the cheese is melted and bubbly.
- Garnish:
  - Sprinkle chopped green onions and sesame seeds over the baked pizza.
- Serve:
  - Slice the Yakitori Beef and Shishito Pepper Pizza into portions and serve hot.

Enjoy the delicious combination of yakitori beef and shishito peppers on your pizza! This fusion dish offers a perfect blend of savory and slightly spicy flavors. Customize with additional toppings or drizzle extra yakitori sauce for an added burst of taste.

www.ingramcontent.com/pod-product-compliance
Lightning Source LLC
LaVergne TN
LVHW061940070526
838199LV00060B/3890